SPECTRAL
LINES

SPECTRAL

LINES

Poems about Scientists

Various Authors

Selected by
Leah Angstman, Laura Brzyski, S. E. Carson,
Summer Kurtz, and Eric Shonkwiler

Curated and Edited by
Leah Angstman

Alternating Current Press
Boulder, Colorado

Spectral Lines
Poems about Scientists
Various Authors
©2019 Alternating Current Press

Alternating Current
Boulder, Colorado
alternatingcurrentarts.com

ISBN-10: 1-946580-08-2
ISBN-13: 978-1-946580-08-5
First Edition: February 2019

Letter from the Editor

At the intersection of science and poetry, strange things happen. There exists such a bizarre human experience and shared understanding, that we can't help but admire and celebrate it. It's transcendent—the crossover of discovery and beauty. The physical solid realism and the ethereal intangible ideas. The inexplicable, the long-desired solutions, the struggle that comes in between. I couldn't have even imagined what we'd find at that intersection, but this anthology is nothing if not transcendent in its own right.

We specifically sought poetry. We specifically sought work on individual scientists, eliminating general themes. We wanted the fundamentals of those scientists—a feeling, an atmosphere, something humanistic that breathes life into their beings, into their work. We plainly stated that we were not seeking "biographies with line breaks." Scientists could be dead or alive, and we viewed "scientist" as a very liberal term that could range anywhere from biologists to computer techs to inventors to chemists to naturalists and beyond.

What we received were some of the most personal pieces we've encountered in our 26 years of publishing. Poets wrote about their microbiologist parents, their role models and mentors, their LGBT kinship with ostracized queerness, the women who've been written out of discoveries, the underdogs overlooked for Nobels. The pieces are searching and full of light, passionate and full of awe. There is such hope and despair on these pages that I was in joy and tears at every turn; I wanted to do something unique to capture this personal experience.

So, I asked each author to write fifty words about his scientist and about his connection to the scientist. Those paragraphs are featured on the pages with the poems and are every bit as fascinating and poetic as the pieces themselves. Rather than regurgitating Wikipedia (which no good researcher wants to do!), I asked the authors to speak in their own words, their own voices. They all complained how hard it was to narrow their role models and passions into fifty words, but the result is that you, the reader, get to see what about each scientist is truly important and impactful to the author, what the true lasting legacy is for each individual, and the personal connections—the elusive *"why"*—that drew each poet to that particular scientist. You become the voyeur both into the scientists' laboratories and into the poets' headspaces.

I tell you, it's transcendent.

Research is what I'm doing
when I don't know what I'm doing.
—Wernher von Braun (1912–1977)

Science is not only a disciple of reason
but also one of romance and passion.
—Stephen Hawking (1942–2018)

Science and everyday life cannot
and should not be separated.
—Rosalind Franklin (1920–1958)

I hadn't been aware
that there were doors closed to me
until I started knocking on them.
—Gertrude B. Elion (1918–1999)

Nothing in the universe can travel at the speed of light, they say,
forgetful of the shadow's speed.
—Howard Nemerov (1920–1991)

We especially need imagination in science.
It is not all mathematics, nor all logic,
but it is somewhat beauty and poetry.
—Maria Mitchell (1818–1889)

And yet, it moves.
—Galileo Galilei (1564–1642)

Table of Contents

Matter

SPECTRAL ⚛ LINES

Poems about Scientists

Warming Up in the Museum of Surgical Science

Kindra McDonald

After the rain-soaked wind off Lake Michigan
blew us in, we read about the miracle of X-Rays.
Our insides reveal another medical mystery in
the shadowy folds of our stomachs.
I watch our reflections in the darkened windows
as we pass, see my heart beat faster as you hold my hand.
The light and dark of our craniums glow like halos.

This magic was catching, a technology for the masses.
The Buster Brown shoe size indicators,
the little phalanges pointing up, a souvenir of your child's
growing foot, radiating confidence so shoes wouldn't be
outgrown by summer's end. Line your little ones up.

With his wife's hand, long-boned with thick joints,
Röntgen presented her photo to the world
and in that first X-Ray she had seen her death,
the future of her grave.

Now I see your back and my hip, your leg and our
ghostly teeth smiling at each other. Our fingers
overlap as you lead me back outside.
Geiger counters beep as we pass, all those cellphones
pressed to bent heads, luminous.

> **Wilhelm Röntgen (1845–1923)**
> was a German Nobel Prize-winning
> physicist who invented the X-Ray. The
> first X-Ray was his wife Anna's hand.
> Her first words after seeing it were, "I
> have seen my death." Many of my loved
> ones have had their trajectories changed
> by the father of diagnostic radiology.

Lower Cambrian

Colleen Maynard

Vija Celmins' velvety prints
of the ocean in the dark

calm;

Ernst Haeckel's monographs of
mollusk and starfish

ignite.

Limestone roadcuts flank
the station wagon on
the Maryland turnpike.
I press my temple against the pane,
nose the air, drop my jaw.
Things arrive and recede.

A dribble of water
shimmers
from a fissure.
A stromatolite inside that rock—
an animal that looks like
a brain pretending to be a cactus—
would mean
this was once tropical sea.

I amuse myself by transforming the drab
lichen lining the Appalachians
into emerald and saffron corals
swaying in the currents.

My grandmother's Virginia Slims
powder out from a box of blouses
sealed ten years ago.

Mr. Haeckel's drawings of calcified corals
(though gaudy as parlor wallpaper)
were attempts to name and colonize
life before humans.

Mr. Audubon rationalized
playing with dead birds
by magnifying, measuring,
and sketching wingspans.

But who's the real genius,
Audubon or the man
who propped up his dead bride,
piling on makeup once her skin
began to go, stabilizing the abscesses
with sawdust and putty?

We roll up the drive, get out of the car.
Stretch and survey.
Our all-American summerhouse is
a coconut ice-cream cake
perched on wicker.
Only the dark under the porch,
held back by latticed slats,
suggests the possibility
of blooming rot.

**John James Audubon
(1785–1851)** created *The Birds
of America*, an illustrated
collection of 700 species that
was produced from earnings of
portrait commissions and
hunted animal skins. Audubon
was an ornithologist and
painter but also a slaveowner,
mine owner, and traveling
salesman whose life was saved
often by his father and wife.
The scientific work of artists
Ernst Haeckel (1834–1919)
and **Vija Celmins (b. 1938)** is
also referenced.

Red Linnaeus

Amy Wright

Uppsala Cathedral: Linnaeus in the tombs
burns beloved common names—his
halo. Long-buried, binomial-ceremonies
Master, cloaked in the foremost romance
language.

Aglow under cut glass, *Melanophila*
acuminata infrared-detects still-warm wood,
Carolus' palm pressed to his wonderstruck chest.

Life is a carcanet. He said, I'll string it, genus
by monosemous species, *nota bene*
idiosyncrasies, glean the spider's silk
dewdrops inside which aphids sway limbs.
A reader in the text I write, I read

wing count and leaf skin, insulate
erythrocytes from every first-look blush,
unknowns swelling under one tongue,
a golden coffin. Tourist,
my order softens into a worshipful
private recital, a chorus, a chant.

> **Carl Linnaeus (1707–1778)** was a
> Swedish botanist, physician, and
> zoologist best known for formalizing
> binomial nomenclature. His work
> helped me recognize that
> taxonomists have much in common
> with poets, who are similarly
> concerned with precisely naming the
> world in an endless effort to better
> understand it.

The scientific name *Melanophila acuminata* refers to a wood-boring beetle commonly known
as the black fire beetle because it is drawn to fire and smoldering cinders.

Trinity

Michael H. Levin

Let not this heat dispirit me
that streams so fierce it blisters skin
past gaps that cover miles
or blinding light that turns the
blue hills white; but then the wind
a dragon's breath that flattens scrub
and banshees on as though to
never end—but then a growl
that rumbles like the heaving earth
might rise, cascading in an
angry swirl to coffin
up scorched observation posts.

Please god, the work was fire: six
years of sweated midnight math,
precision grinding, shouted
disagreements while our soup
or scrambled eggs grew cold. The
path Prometheus took, made new.
What batters now no witness
on this Dead Men's Trail dares say.
Ears plugged, we brace with stunned
relief against the booming
air—exhale, and glance away.

This poem is told from the
composite perspective of Manhattan
Project members who witnessed the
first atomic explosion, named
Trinity, from Dead Men's Trail near
Los Alamos (July 1945). Many
Project members developed second
thoughts about nuclear energy after
the first controlled chain reaction
(Chicago Pile-1, December 1942).

Domestication

Catharina Coenen

"You are responsible, forever, for what you have tamed,"
the fox said to the little prince.

Temple Grandin loved
to lay on her back in a field with cattle
until the sky above her face filled with circles
of horns
and calm, curious eyes. She spent her life designing
curved ramps and chutes to help them amble
unhurried, unafraid
to the quick metal or electric bolt.

Nikolai Vavilov died
in prison, in the midst of war,
slowly, of starvation,
for speaking of genes determining destiny,
dangerous thoughts gathered with potatoes, beets, and grains
from farmers in the Andes and the Fertile Crescent.
The scientists he left behind in Leningrad walked the rooftops
of his institute with guns, defending from a starving city
ten thousand years of tending—
the seeds and thoughts and tubers
that would feed the Russian peasants and
the world
in a future of diseases, drought, and cold.
By the time the siege was broken,
nine of them had starved to death on insufficient rations
between carefully catalogued bags
of barley, wheat, and rye.

And I spoon
on the linoleum
under the veterinarian's table
against the cooling body
of my dog, who,
in his tenth year of life, the ninth of our belonging,
bit my neighbor's face.

"What does that mean—'tame,'" asked the little prince.
"It is an act too often neglected," said the fox.
"It means to establish ties."

Temple Grandin (b. 1947) is a professor of animal science at Colorado State University. She is known for her books on autism and on animal behavior. **Nikolai Ivanovich Vavilov (Николай Иванович Вавилов, 1887–1943)** was a Russian botanist and geneticist, who directed the world's largest seed bank. He was sentenced to death for criticizing the theories of Stalin's minister of agriculture.

the short distance ahead

Robin Gow

dear Alan Turing, forgive me
for remaking your machine, the first
approximation of a computer with its
stripe of paper & 0/1 number-making.
i won't pretend to know what it's for,
but i'm told that it answers questions.
i ask myself if i write poetry for
the same reasons you took up a love
of numbers. in a video about your life
they claim you sought out truth
& i laughed because people always assume
the numbers will be sturdy for us—that we
can trust them to hold on to. take the number 6:
the number of war-years & the number of men
who left their thumbprints on your neck.
i want to meet you out on the front green
at Cambridge, a notebook in your lap
as you write equations like love poetry.
what is the number bigger than all other numbers?
i ask your machine & it writes a sonnet
about the end of the second world war
& your code-breaking calculations.
oh, we all know that heroes are stalwart like
numbers. are impermeable. the backroom
where you promised not to attempt making
truth out of his body—you told him
that no one could ever ever know. i called
my brother last night & told him about
you. i asked him if he knew that the man
who made the first computer was gay & then i said
that it's not fair to put the weight of our
words on people long passed.
my brother listened & the machine
kept going, trying to make sense of
words between brothers. i wrote your
quote on the top of my notebook:
we can only see a short distance ahead,
but we can see plenty there that needs to
be done &
i see you staring hard at the floor

of the doctor's office as they give you
your first shot of estrogen, the homosexual cure.
i told my brother this was what they did
to gay men in England, the feminine
hormone to make malleable bodies, to make
antidote of a heart. i feel guilty because
when i take hormones they arrange a man
out of me. i'm thinking of my own short
distance ahead & the machine on
the countertop. until i met you i
distrusted the numbers, always.
i saw them as a false sense of absolute—
the inarguable marble gods: the 14, the 15,
the 16, the years i spent raging inside skin.
why do we fight our bodies like this?
why do they fight our bodies for us?
the spot on the wall you look at as your
body takes in the estrogen each week.
weeping on the end of the bed, numbers
written all across your body as if they
could right the wrongs inflicted on you.
the machine is giving me 0s, which
means no no no no no
every time i eat an apple, i think
of the one you bit full of your own cyanide.
i tell my brother that i read history
not because i think i can ever right a wrong
but maybe i can resurrect it, cut it open,
give it numbers.

Alan Turing (1912–1954) was a founding theorist
behind computer science. He was also instrumental
in deciphering coded messages Nazis were sending
during World War II. Turing died by suicide after
he admitted to being "homosexual," which was a
crime in the U.K. at that time. As a young queer
person, I think it's important to know his story.

Signed, with compliments of the Surgeon-General of the Army,

Leah Angstman

Rewind from the metastases in pleura, nodules rapidly later
but slowly first appearing at the vertical scar,
vertebral border of scapula—that jargon.
Rewind that jargon to carcinoma at inferior angles of upper joints,
where arm and clavicle left as you watched,
amputated from the shoulder. Rewind before that.

Gold Rush. We know that time; we are Americans here.
Brought your father from Austria to daunting California hills,
a boom agent of Wells, Fargo, and Company.
You were born into our yellow fever.
Yet, your mother's fever you'd follow: medical science
once called upon by Ferdinand Maximilian.

Röntgen-rays, these fascinating things.
Partner the man who fascinated you into them,
then continue without him and into the gadgets of pretty words:
fluoroscopes and radiographs. *How pretty science is.*
Lie on the table and snap rays of yourself, or of him,
of him and of yourself, in turns.
See the result after twenty minutes; rest in this box
for one hour, two; rest in a box for five years, eternity.
How quick the manifestations of acute radiodermatitis,
lesions of black-gray split into pronounced red veinwork.
At its worst, pus lapped against char.

How unpretty science is. The Presidio spilled over with
American war bodies boated in from the Philippines,
and yours was to unlodge Mauserheads and capture skull damage,
intercostal spaces, in grays. You did this without protection
to ease patients. (Women feared it could undress them at will—
perish the thought!) Show that science is painless.
That rash is from something unrelated.
Just sit here. Lie back. *I promise, I promise.*

There is no rewinding now.
We are here, where we've arrived in a short life.
Arrived to jargon that does not ease patience:
ulcerated tissues over the middle phalanges, necrogenica,
branching papilloma, nodule through epithelium, epidermoid carcinoma.
Amputate, Elizabeth; you must.
Hear me now, through the ages: *you must.*
Your head shakes, and I can see how it must have shook.
That will is yours, and for half the year.
Destruction of secretion glands and hair follicles—
nothing grows and flows here. Amputate.

DEATH OF A FAMOUS WOMAN RADIOGRAPHER,
signed obituary decrees, *came as a relief.*
From a sepia dog-eared corner,
Elizabeth shakes her head.

**Elizabeth Fleischmann-Aschheim
(1867–1905)** was a Jewish-American
radiographer, an X-Ray pioneer who
removed bullets from skulls during the
Philippine-American War, and the
first woman to die from X-Ray effects,
after experimenting on her own body.
She opened California's first X-Ray
laboratory and was instrumental in
developing the lead sheets we still
wear for radiation protection today.

Rutherford Discovers His Own Hollowness

Armin Tolentino

*It was quite the most incredible event
that has ever happened to me in my life.*

—Ernest Rutherford

I shoot gold skin with alpha flecks that flake from radium's
face, a collapse into lead and vanishing blue. If elements,

as Thomson claims, are cities of sprawling charges—
an even scatter of plus and minus—then these particles

will carom and veer through gold as wind slants
English rain. Shocked, I watch one hundred thousand

subatomic bullets pass the foil undeterred, their path
direct and confident as Newton's writing hand.

Daylight succumbs to the urge of horizon, but I remain
in a dark lab, rubbing my wedding band. What we call

precious, I now know, is only luster and empty space.

Ernest Rutherford (1871–1937) was a
New Zealand-born chemist who
conducted the gold foil experiments
that revolutionized our understanding
of atomic structure. Instead of the **J. J.
Thomson (1856–1940)** Plum Pudding
Model, we now accept the Rutherford
Model: a dense, positively charged
nucleus surrounded by nearly massless
electrons and empty space in between.

Rainbow Streamers

Jane Frank

after Sir Isaac Newton's Opticks: or, a Treatise
of the Reflexions, Refractions, Inflexions
and Colours of Light, *1704*

I'm looking back at you through a telescope that magnifies
early notebooks crammed with recipes for paint,
medicines, and instructions for clever conjuring tricks

You could magic windmills run by live mice and build
remarkable sundials at a young age, but making friends
was the branch of science that challenged you most so
instead you wrote ten million secret words

Born under a Christmas star, you documented all the deadly
sins you could remember, a straight discourse with God—
the rages and dark depressions that would blight your life

You were first to know the rainbow, the ROYGBIV
colors that, seen through a prism, make up the spectrum,
but you had suffered your mother's rejection, betrayals,
and a nervous breakdown before you saw the light ...

... that narrow portion within the electromagnetic spectrum
that can be seen by the human eye, the selective absorption
that overturned the dogma of the sun's "pureness"

As you swim now in a multiverse where waves don't
travel in straight lines, we widen grateful eyes: lives open
to streams of sensation curated by our minds

> **Sir Isaac Newton (1642–1727)** was an English
> physicist, mathematician, astronomer, and great mind
> of the Scientific Revolution. He created the telescope,
> the laws of motion and gravitation, and my subject
> here—spectral analysis—understanding and
> identifying the seven colors of the rainbow, which
> means much to me as a lover of art and words.

Decayed Ghazal

Sara Sams

The law of conservation of parity was wrong, Chien-Shiung proved so.
The men she proved so for won the Nobel Prize for Chien-Shiung.

A novelty calendar teaches me her name; she helped us fuel the bomb
    and understand decay.
Inherently likeable in its cobalt furs, Chien-Shiung's beta decay

says *scintillator* and yet stays far away from issues of consent.
Conservation of parity trusted nature to be symmetrical, in agreement

with itself; how like a mime you raise your glass and I raise mine,
how in the mirror I'm berating myself berating myself, uniformly,

only we're zoomed way in now, and I never took physics. I always wanted
my head spun round in other ways. But now I want

to know: is there a problem to chew on so tasty
I might, to my very last, doubt? I want to see my mouth

still puckering, *cosmological constant* a candy on my tongue
by a board where two fat balls bob the thought of particles.

Don't they look like surly clowns? I think they would laugh,
if they could, at their jumbo size, their chalky solidity,

at my funny little need to know, and me,
plumbing me, still, up until the very last.

Wu Chien-Shiung (吳健雄, 1912–1997) was a Chinese-born American physicist who, in addition to making other important contributions to our understanding of particle physics, worked to develop the process of separating uranium metal into uranium isotopes for gaseous diffusion. This diffusion process was replicated at the K-25 plant in my hometown, Oak Ridge, Tennessee, in order to develop fuel for the atomic bomb.

Petite Curies

Kathy Ackerman

What good is this gold?
The Bank of France refuses it—
they've melted heirlooms, rings, and crowns to fund the war,
but my Nobel they reject, as though to melt it
is a greater crime than surgeons guessing where to cut.

I've nothing left to give to this war,
my prize money spent on bonds,
my apartment filled with sewing machines,
my own daughter ruining her bones on battlefields.

They call my X-Ray cars *Petite Curies*,
like they are fashionable desserts, to serve with demitasse.
Would they call them such if Pierre were driving them?
At the Front, Irène was brave as any soldier.

It is criminal to deny to us the Croix de Guerre,
the one prize I would cherish
for its metal—bronze, not gold,
and crossed by swords.

> **Marie Curie (1867–1934)** won two
> Nobel Prizes for her extraordinary
> work with radium and polonium. She
> also invented a portable X-Ray car that
> she used on the battlefields in World
> War I. Those of us who have lost
> loved ones to cancer know that
> radiation is both a blessing and a curse.

Concerning the Two New Sciences

Matilda Berke

That the sundog is an optical illusion
    should come as no surprise.
Who would hew new heavens
    from diamond dust, a few
mortal words & stained-glass leaves
    ten meters deep? Not me.
I'd gladly flee these worlds for a bit of
    peace & quiet,
so I say it's better this way. Being not-all-knowing.
    I raised a spyglass to the sky
& my rosary became a string of beads.
    I must confess
I never quite learned how to pray;
    you see, they couldn't stop me poking
points of light between the verses,
    though I really think He would've liked them.
It's a funny thing. Strike the mouth of a man
    & call it God—the cry in the night, the hunter
streaked over a welkin plate. I am only a scholar.
    Trust me when I say I know a love
more holy than the moon. Trust me the first time.
    So much is purer unmagnified:
the sun, the stars, a man gone blind
    for lack of sky. Dropping cannonballs
like so many counterfeit auroras, dropping
    cannonballs to keep these fingers warm.

Galileo Galilei (1564–1642), called "the father of
the scientific method," was infamous for
championing Copernican heliocentrism. Because this
theory contradicted the Church's dogma, he was
investigated by the Roman Inquisition and placed
under house arrest for life, where he wrote *Dialogues
Concerning Two New Sciences* (summarizing his
findings regarding material strength) but was forced
to recant earlier astronomical conclusions.

Kumara Chips

Harvey Aughton

Sweet potatoes are cut into wedges the world over
Deep-fried and sold in paper bags or wrapped in news
Strains of kumara are divided in Oceania, by island
Destined for mangroves, volcanic soil and temperate
Zones where headlines talk of the price of chip dinners
But should they talk, in bold letters, of the woman
Who brought completion from the sky, from high
In the tropics and propagated the finest kumara
Under the sun and rain, in wind and snow, on Aotearoa

> **Whakaotirangi (c. 1300s)** is considered Aotearoa's first scientist. She ensured the safe transport of kumara, a tropical vegetable, to Aotearoa. She is also credited with innovative horticultural methods that ensured kumara's success in a new, colder, and more volatile climate. It's important to me that we recognize scientific achievements from periods before the enlightened European advent of Natural Philosophy.

The Astronomer

Amanda Bloom

They ask if the flag can be seen,
perhaps with our strongest telescope.
Or the footprints, as though
the moon is a silent bell
and man
the hammer,
as though nothing happened before
and nothing has happened since.

Do I tell them we are the nothing,
the universe is expanding
always, maybe,
and us
forever smaller inside, if
we were to stand in the middle
of a crater,
mountains, all around,
would cut the black sky?

The moon has yet to settle
into perfect orbit.
It is leaving us each year
by the half-inch; it is barely
even ours.

Scott MacNeill (b. 1975) is Staff Astronomer at Brown University's Ladd Observatory, Director of Frosty Drew Observatory in Rhode Island, and a software engineer. His writing and astronomical photographs appear in *BBC Sky at Night*, *Space.com*, *EarthSky*, and elsewhere. I heard Scott answer questions about the moon while I was visiting Frosty Drew.

Gertrude Caton Thompson in Egypt

Wilda Morris

Flinders Petrie assigned me
quarters in a nobleman's tomb
emptied out in Roman times.
I shared it, not with mummies
or other archeologists,
but with a family of cobras.
They slept by day
while I sorted artifacts
and searched a wadi
for Paleolithic remains.
At night when I slept,
the cobras went out to hunt.
Did I kill them? you ask. How could I?
That tomb had been their family home
for generations. I was the trespasser.

Gertrude Caton Thompson (1888–1985)
developed archeological techniques that were
well ahead of her time. She made important
discoveries in Egypt and Malta, and, at a
time when many Europeans did not believe
Africans capable of creating great
civilizations, she demonstrated that Great
Zimbabwe had been built by native Africans.
I admire her work and her courage.

Kepler's Last Autumn

Steve Wilson

> *Mensus eram coelos, nunc terrae metior umbras*
> *Mens coelestis erat, corporis umbra iacet.*
> —Kepler's self-penned epitaph

Imagine, I can't comprehend
what I see. It's all erosion and false-

shape of shadow—leaves me undone.
Explanations incomplete, journeys

abandoned midway over the mountains.
You expect the insight of sages, a silvered charm

that spirits us past chasms where
hollow takes hold. Know: trees stumble

through my nights same as yours. Oceans open.
Planets, memories, systems spin round

that moment we'll first know our minds.
If I promised, I've failed. If I loved you,

I regret. How we wander through loss,
following traces cut across the horizon.

> **Johannes Kepler (1571–1630)**
> expressed a charmingly aesthetic
> sense of the cosmos through his
> belief that the movement of
> celestial bodies created heavenly
> music. I hope to explore the
> doubts Kepler, a poetic scientist,
> faced as his health slowly failed,
> and his confidence in his
> observations was sorely tested by
> his approaching death.

The Robbery of Rosalind Franklin

Carol Barrett

for Anne Sayre

You tell us lost facts
are not always replaceable:
biography too cruel

a word for a life
spiraling into oblivion.
Watson? A very fine art

to be persuasive so briefly,
post-mortem, at that.
You broke the phantom

spectacles his ego invented,
led us to the plain light
that was hers, sketching

a landscape in perspective
at the age of eight,
the carpenter's bench

for fine dovetail
and miter. What she touched
she adorned. In crystallography,

in graphite, in carbons,
her goal: illuminate
elusive structure.

She followed a line
of prophets: Isaiah
planted selective seeds.

Mendel mixed the smooth-skinned
and the wrinkled. His peas
have fourteen chromosomes.

Horses, 64. (Did Watson
get more than his share?)
In a widow's room, bookshelves

crowned with statuary
to fit the ceiling, Rosalind
bartered lessons in French

conjugations and cooking.
Frame and beauty, her guides.
Sugar rationed, she longed

for sticky cakes, not
the Irish pub in the Strand
where they primed

her assistant for the curled
threads of her work. Watson claims
she came from behind

the lab bench to assault him.
He was the assailant, attributing
the discovery he needed

he would use—the location
of the sugar-phosphate
backbone of the molecule

on the outside looking in,
as Rosalind must, outside,
look in—to the outpourings

of a misguided feminist.
She was robbed. The rest
of her life she dismantled

viruses in an old house
bombed in the war, afterward
cobbled together. Her beakers

and pots caught the drips,
room on the fifth floor,
the last stairs twisted

against the wall. She refused
cancer's tourniquet, needling
deadly polio in the cellar.

Of Watson's stealth Rosalind
was innocent, never asked,
nor guessed, never was told.

Watson's one regret:
she didn't build better models.
He liked a noisy burial.

The moral of his story:
winner take all. Of yours:
let us unsilence her life.

Rosalind Franklin (1920–1958)
discovered the helical structure of
DNA. Working without the support
enjoyed by her male colleagues, and
contributing to the uncovery of the
genetic code, she died before **James
Watson (b. 1928)**, who with cohort
Francis Crick (1916–2004) received
the Nobel Prize for the work,
published *The Double Helix*,
describing a woman he called
"Rosy" with disdain and deceit. To
correct the record, **Anne Sayre
(1923–1998)** wrote *Rosalind Franklin
and DNA*. I was chagrined to learn in
Sayre's biography that once again,
men were given credit for work
achieved by a woman scientist.

Inventions

Lorraine Schein

When whiting-out
the sky's typos
your brush-tip blobbed
with the liquid paper moon,
remember Bette Nesmith Graham—
who, after inventing
Monkee Mike Nesmith,
invented it.

She was an artist who
had to be a secretary
but was a lousy typist.

One day she took some
white tempera paint
and a watercolor brush
to the office
to cover her mistakes.

Soon her fellow secretaries
were clamoring for it.

> **Bette Nesmith Graham
> (1924–1980)** was the
> mother of Mike Nesmith of
> The Monkees and inventor
> of Liquid Paper correction
> fluid. As a baby boomer
> and office worker, I was
> familiar with both. After
> reading a book about
> women inventors, I was
> inspired to write about
> Graham and also the less
> successful, quirky
> inventions of other women.

So she put some into
a green mustard bottle
she found at home,
wrote "Mistake Out" on a label,
and Liquid Paper was born.

But other women's inventions didn't take:
The self-cleaning house,
The electronic Bible,
Mrs. Ritter's expandable jockstrap.

The sun hat for horses,
The dog spectacles,
The parakeet diapers of Bertha Dlugi.

Silliness is the daughter of invention.

Imprinting

Jessica Conley

I was born with a mark on my
palm easily mistaken for a burn.
I have a filial affection for might-
be flames, but that I can touch
and take as mine: a mountain fire
bush's new leaves, a Persian silk
tree's fibrous blooms, a red bulb

to warm the quail eggs that hatched
in a lab. My father reared them,
fed them red cactus pear, taught
them what choices to make. When
offered cascara and assorted larvae,
they hesitated at the lack of color.
*Developing adaptive preferences from
birth*, he titled the paper. His students
broke the quails' necks, plucked their
scaled feathers for a feast, ripping
the birds' thin skin in a rush to be rid

of their plumage. Hypothesis: I would
make a beautiful feathered creature.

My mother, the microbiologist,
anatomized *Martha Stewart Living's*
yearly Halloween edition, Martha's
Spooky Scary Sounds screeching
through the boombox. To chimerical
wailing and offbeat creaking, I chose
the most flammable. An organza
ghost. A matador with her cape.
The year I was a raven, I spray-
painted my hair black; the enamel
webbed the strands inseparable.
My muslin feathers brushed against
walkways' paper lanterns lit dim

and dangerous. If my wings caught
fire, a bevy of hands palming the grass
for a hose slick and black in the dark
could only save what remained of me—
singed wire too heavy for flight.

Stephen Burton (b. 1956) and
Cynthia Burton (b. 1958) are
my parents. They studied sleep
psychology and microbiology,
respectively. My father
explored factors that shape
dreams, and my mother
worked in a laboratory
identifying and determining
appropriate treatment for
diseases. Their roles as
scientists created a lens through
which I view myself and my
relationships with others.

Taikonauts

Megan Gieske

2015: The sun's magnetic field is about to flip,
and mercury is in retrograde. 2014: Heaven's
in the Pleiades. 2010: The total lunar eclipse,
and the winter solstice. 2003: *Columbia's*
suspended in orbit with me, and we're as silent
as a supernova. 1993: Hubble's first photographs,
blurred by stars condensed like water.
1989: All the Earth swoons at Venus.
1984: Two Chinese taikonauts

lost to light and space tethered to each other
like twins to the apparatus of our orbit,
listen to the pull of our Mother's gravity
on strips of polyester balloons, the ragged
flags on satellites, fruit flies with parachutes,
Rhesus monkeys, and Laika, a Siberian Samoyed
from the streets of Moscow with famous winter,
all in an ardent capsule.

During the Dragon Boat Festival, they toss dumplings
into rivers on Saturn's moon, Titan, so cosmic fish
won't nibble on the poet Qu Yuan. Like Armstrong,
they each shut one eye, the shadows of their thumbs
holding distances between things, the blackened Earth,
there in the full moonlight with lunar reflection
and solar clarity, ethereal, sobering, and misgiving.

Beneath global beauty, Asia's blue touched with red
like the palates of the Four Great Masters,
they recite a Chinese tale of those about to cause harm
who, when beholding beauty, could only love and cherish,
becoming protectors instead of violators.

> **Liu Yang (劉洋, b. 1978)** and **Wang Yaping (王亞平, b.
> 1980)** are the first Chinese women in space. Liu became
> the first Chinese woman in space in 2012, with Wang
> following closely behind her in 2013. The poem
> references the rumored *Taikonauts* lost in space, but it is
> dedicated to these two courageous women.

The Chemist, 1934

Carl Boon

Fear green when the Bunsen's hot—
we are not children given to tropical
glows. We must be wary; we must avoid
breathing it, washing it, emerald thallium,
even though these lab's low windows
display April outside, April of daffodil
stems, of Christ and life beginning again
all orchestra-radiant.

I am a chemist. I deal in what remains,
and somehow carry everything inside,
an arsenic trace, a radium wish, need
for a woman who doesn't love me. I arrange
my body against my tables and books,
and smooth my tie with the capacity
of a stranger. They call me when
the world they call romantic goes awry.

I love Mathilda secretly, yet surmise
that love is a composition, too, to rise
inside of us and decompose. To glow
on August days and then recede—my hair,
my fingernails, my skin.
If there is a Savior, maybe He, too,
recedes, a stranger in a New York breadline,
and precisely one of us, at last.

Walking in Brooklyn I watch a child dance—
I watch her limbs that will be carbon.
I watch her mother coax her
with pink, alluring glucose. I am stable.
I am a chemist. I call to Mathilda to come,
let's have a drink of water
and dance before the world dissects us,
before I'm abandoned to my scales.

> **Alexander Gettler
> (1883–1968)** was a New
> York toxicologist who,
> together with **Charles
> Norris (1867–1935)**,
> developed the art of
> forensic chemistry as a
> means of criminal
> justice. Gettler figures
> prominently in Deborah
> Blum's *The Poisoner's
> Handbook*, which was
> made popular by the
> 2014 PBS *American
> Experience* film of the
> same name.

Heisenberg and Bohr

Christie Wilson

In the hours of the day
when light gathers and fans,
dispersing itself on the
lawn, soaking down through
grass and dirt, into walls and
all that separates the living quarters
of Heisenberg and Bohr,
they argue.

The things that divide us!
Each man,
at uncertain moments,
in uncertain spaces,
thinks.

Bohr's pacing,
wine wavelike in his veins,
signals open shores for particles
to arrive or appear.

Youth, as it sometimes does,
forces Heisenberg to abhor
contradiction to pattern he has only
just mastered, has used to light his way.

The irony of the boy finding the matrix,
as if it were just there among the rocks,
of finding the rules
only to discover the rules
rule out certainty.

But the whole of that comes later
and he reconciles, yes.
Heisenberg and Bohr will sit together again,
stand side by side undergirding
what becomes the modern version
of all the versions to come.

Though, right now, in the now that is these words,
the hope comes not from the future.
Rather, it seeps from exhaustion,
from ground defended in concept and name,
from the departure of Bohr, leaving Heisenberg
to fold in on himself,
and begin again.

Niels Bohr (1885–1962) and **Werner Heisenberg (1901–1976)** were both recipients of the Nobel Prize in Physics. Bohr was a mentor to Heisenberg, hosting Heisenberg at his institute where they argued through ideas such as the Uncertainty Principle and the Complementarity Principle. I was fascinated to learn how their relationship shaped the foundations of quantum mechanics.

Henry S. Kaplan

Roger Sippl

In 1979, Henry S. Kaplan won the Kettering Prize
for medical research excellence, and a life
of bringing his gentlemanly manner
to bear on the hardest problem.

The award was for being the master of intellectual daring,
in small rooms, with large machines,
pointing heavy beams of X-Rays,
almost enough to kill, and later,
nitrogen mustard drugs in the veins …

… so that with an arrogance only
excusable in supreme righteousness,
he could say, "It's cured."

I had wished for him the Nobel
Prize, but then I wished the next greater compensation,
yet now, remembering the man,
I know he had it all along.

Henry S. Kaplan (1918–1984) is the
father of modern-day radiation
therapy, particularly applied to
curing people with Hodgkin's
Lymphoma, which was nearly
always fatal before his work. He was
my doctor. I was accepted into his
clinic at Stanford in 1974, when I
was a 19-year-old pre-med at UC
Berkeley with Stage IIIB Hodgkin's.

Elemental

Charles Kersey

This world of silicon and golden trace,
though often one of logic: stone and cold
where dreams are traded: faded, lost and sold,
is sometimes blessed with purity and grace.

Systemic elements so dull, so base,
the molecules that make up board and flesh
in clean room lab or chromosomal crèche,
so delicately merge within your face ...

Organic synergetic interface!
Each separate feature beautiful in part
more dazzling still when mixed with soul and heart.
The light and warmth of suns your eyes outpace!

The power of the pasts you hold by will
within your eyes. So elemental still ...

Lise Meitner (1878–1968) was an
Austrian-Swedish physicist. Alongside
Otto Hahn (1879–1968) and **Otto Frisch
(1904–1979)**, Meitner led a group of
scientists who discovered uranium fission
in 1939. The 1944 Nobel Prize in
Chemistry went to Hahn, excluding
Meitner and Frisch. Her epitaph by Frisch
reads: "Lise Meitner, a physicist who
never lost her humanity."

Triptych of a Scientist-Cleric's Legacy

Hannah Carr-Murphy

I.

The first anatomist to describe
the clitoris
was Gabriele Falloppio,
a canon of the Church
in the 16th century,
when, miles of ocean away
Juan Diego was visited
in Guadeloupe.
Did Gabriele breathe *salves*
over that holy mystery
before taking down his notes?

II.

Exactly 1,100 men
participated in the first
clinical trial of condoms
in preventing the spread
of syphilis.
Gabriele Falloppio
called God to witness
that not one man was infected.

The clergy of the 20th century,
called to witness
the suffering of AIDS,
and distribute lifesaving
prophylactics,
covered their eyes.

III.

Today, far from where Falloppio walked
in the Golden Age of Anatomy,
a young woman is crying
over ectopic pregnancy,
where the embryo attaches
outside the uterus,
usually in a tube
that bears his name.
Not crying because her pregnancy
is ectopic, but because it isn't,
leaving the legal drugs
that cause miscarriage
out of her reach
in Holy Ireland,
the Isle of Saints & Scholars.

Gabriele Falloppio (1523–1562)
was a Catholic clergyman, doctor,
and anatomist whose work proving
the effectiveness of the condom to
prevent the spread of disease is
conspicuously absent in
biographies of him published by the
Catholic Church.

Steinmetz on the
Maid of Mists with Friends

Alan Catlin

Dressed in yellow rain slickers
they are four grown men reduced to
childlike routines, fighting imbalances
induced by river currents, eruptions
of waves, the spray from the Canadian
Falls dripping from the bills of their
gear, half-hearted smiles a sign of unease
here except for the small man, childlike
but for the trimmed mustache
and beard. Clearly, he is the most secure,
almost serene on this outing, feeling as if
these unruly elements, these forces are
to be harnessed or contained, converted into
a kind of practical magic, electrical impulses
well beyond the scope of this still life,
well beyond those small dark eyes, looking out,
looking beyond the wet, clinging mists.

Charles Steinmetz (1865–1923) developed the idea
for alternating current, leading the way for the
dissemination of electrical power, and devised
mathematical theories applicable to engineering, a
field my uncle and grandfather worked in. I admire
people who overcome obstacles in life; Steinmetz was
physically disabled, with a hunched back, hip
dysplasia, and dwarfism, but what a mind! When he
died, he had 200 patents to his credit, and he lived in
the city where I reside, Schenectady, New York.

"Ève of the Radium Eyes"

Kathy Ackerman

They believe my mother loves me less
because I'll never win a Nobel Prize,
because my arts are the frivolous ones—music,
fashion, literature, and friends.
They assume she thinks I am less than Irène
who stood beside her at the Front while still a teen,
to show the surgeons where the bullets were.

They assume my mother failed with me, had only love enough
for one—the one who behaves just like our father—
so many have said they see him in her face and her demeanor,
even Mé—but it was Mé who bought the piano for me
and Mé who wanted me to play
and who, despite her scolding about my "stilts" and backless dresses,
my blush and shadow,
asks me at the end of my evenings out,
Did you dance, my dear?

> **Marie Curie (1867–1934)** was a mother as
> well as a Nobel-winning scientist. Her
> oldest daughter, **Irène Joliot-Curie (1897–
> 1956)**, followed in her footsteps and became
> the second woman to win a Nobel Prize in
> science, but Marie's younger daughter, **Ève
> Curie (1904–2007)**, a ravishing beauty, was
> drawn to music and writing. In some ways
> Ève is the most intriguing Curie.

St. Petersburg, 1969

Sherre Vernon

> *Люблю тебя, Петра творенье,*
> *Люблю твой строгий, стройный вид*
> —Пушкин А. С., "Медный всадник"

Yevtushenko lost the Oxford Chair
to Fuller. I remember *Bratsk Station*
yellowing on my bookshelf
and that Sarah said he'd made a pass
on his way through Syracuse.

How I know so few poets
and sleep through Stravinsky.
The way Cyril seared my handwriting
to church domes and rail lines.
How I didn't drink Russia until after the vodka

had left me. It's been ten years. Thirteen. I didn't
buy the Yevtushenko there, but poems
from a street vendor—and I spoke them,
despite you: thirty pounds in my bag
and I bore them from Moscow
to Peter's city, without Pushkin.

Did I tell you, he sneaked me in?
Boiled beets and cutlets
on a Bunsen burner at the Polytechnic.
We lost his birthday glove
near the Kunstkamera. We went back.
I love you Peter's creation.

I loved your father, too.

> **Peter N. Lavrenko (Петер Н. Лавренко, 1943–2007)** was a Soviet physicist who pioneered the use of gravitational fields to study polymers. He rejected the 1990s exodus of his homeland to remain a scientist in Russia's barren halls of academia. Peter's ability to see into the heart of things gave him a profound compassion for vulnerable creatures, including me.

De Motu Cordis
(On the Motion of the Heart)

Heather Combe

> *We have yet to explain, however, in what manner the blood*
> *finds its way back to the heart from the extremities by the veins,*
> *and how and in what way these are the only vessels that convey*
> *the blood from the external to the central parts.*
> —William Harvey, *On the Motion*
> *of the Heart and Blood in Animals*

Her slender arm is clasped in his hand.
One finger softly brushes translucent skin,
feeling her fluttering pulse quicken.
Tracing fragile veins, from elbow to wrist.

Part of him longs to take a scalpel,
and part her skin, like stage curtains.
Hungering to explore her circulation;
to reveal the intricacies of her anatomy.

She shudders. Picturing again the animals,
still breathing, splayed in his study.
The mewling cries, the scalpel's glint;
his notebooks full of precise sketches.

An intense stare and narrowed eyes,
her husband, pathologically curious.
Enslaved to the pursuit of *Knowledge*,
that most insatiable mistress.

Despite herself, she craves these moments.
The unexpected thrill of his gentle touch,
the novelty of his breath on her neck,
and the subtle warmth of his skin on hers.

Too soon, he will return to his research.
Immersed again, in miniature anatomical worlds.
And with heavy heart she will wait, hopeful,
that one day he will find his way home.

**William Harvey
(1578–1657)** was an
English physician who
was the first to describe
the circulatory system
in *An Anatomical Exercise
on the Motion of the Heart
and Blood in Animals*,
referred to as *De Motu
Cordis*. He married
Elizabeth Browne, the
daughter of Elizabeth
I's physician, which is
likely to have furthered
his medical career.

Alternatives to Spruce

Ilan Mochari

I. The Orphan

Daughter: Mother, I'm so glad we can talk this way
while our bubblegum cools.
Tell me: what became of Santa Anna?

Mother: He lost a leg
defending Veracruz from French attack.
He retired from the field
to a life of politics and paper pushing.
In his early seventies, he still raged like a young man
to avenge his loss to the French
who, for their part, had installed
Maximilian as Mexico's puppet ruler.
Santa Anna plotted an insurgency, seeking U.S. support.
The U.S. said *no thanks—but we'll keep you alive.*
We'll grant you asylum in New York City;
just let us know when you plan to arrive.

Daughter: Wow! Only years after the Civil War
had ended. And let me guess:
now there's a park in the Queens town of your upbringing
named for Santa Anna! Or perhaps not a park
but a subway stop or a public fountain
on an uptown block; a boat-filled port
or a rust-green statue; a peeling mural by the mall,
or a shrub like a terebinth near City Hall!

Mother: You've been watching too many musicals, I fear
but this man, Santa Anna, never set foot in
my native Queens. Though New York City was his place of asylum,
and though he had the wealth of a man of means,
our government stashed him on Staten Island.

Daughter: What did he do with his days and nights?

Mother: I'm not sure, but here's what I know:
on Staten Island, there was an orphan grown older,
who ran a glass store that was something like
the neighborhood hangout, not far from the ferry dock.
This orphan, a self-taught camera expert,
served in Lincoln's war as a Yankee photographer;
the troops sent his portraits home to their families.
After the war, more design, more devices:
a feedbag for horses, a burner for Kerosene lamps,
neither a commercial success;
so he opened his glass shop one block from the ferry dock;
his neighbors and customers regaled him
with their own ideas for his industrious talents;
and the orphan truly listened—while perusing Bessemer's patents.

Daughter: Let me guess who one of these neighbors was.

Mother: No skipping ahead, my impatient one.
Besides, digressions are where the fun is.
The distaste for discourse is the sign
of the mind ill-suited for the most honest stories
and of the brain too intoxicated by life's pragmatic poisons:
the arbitrary symbols (time, money)
that for too many humans seem like the whiteness of the whale
rather than the commonplace colors of narrower perceptions.

Daughter: But I'm not wrong! Am I?
One of the neighbors must have been Santa Anna.

Mother: Strictly speaking, one of the neighbors
was Santa Anna's proxy.
The proxy told the orphan there was big money in tires—
automobiles were the future.
Automobiles were the new photography.
"And all you need to make the tires
on which a nation of cars will greatly depend,
is a bountiful supply of cheap resin,
access to which is in the hands
of a privileged, famous Mexican—
Santa Anna's his name: ever heard of him?
You'll win customers on price, and on quality, too.
All you need is the resin—so what will you do?
Tomorrow I'll bring Santa Anna to you."

Daughter: Mother, it seems you like musicals, too!

Mother: The singsong rhymes offset my blues,
but let's get on with the story
lest I fail to amuse:
Santa Anna, grown older,
still pining for glory,
rang for the orphan the very next morn.
And before the orphan could say hello,
Santa Anna began in the form of a song:

> *I, said the General, am Napoleon of the West;*
> *speak loudly to me for I'm partially deaf.*
> *Though my hair is white, and I walk with a cane,*
> *my virility trampled a mulatto slave.*
> *She screamed my name proudly, pulled my hair,*
> *and I was the king of the whole hemisphere.*
> *To reclaim my nation by violence and force*
> *is my fate—I'll achieve it, as a monarch I'll die.*
> *You'll help me raise money and profit yourself*
> *making tires from chicle I cheaply supply.*

Daughter: What a pitch.
I'm guessing they reached an agreement.

Mother: Indeed.

Importing one ton of Yucatán chicle with the General's capital,
the orphan worked with his sons in the lab, for months,
attempting to morph the sticky sap into something, anything
resembling tire-like rubber.
But his skilled, subtle, heuristic hands,
ever seeking to master the most challenging crafts,
to obtain the hard-won knowledge of the self-taught artisan,
could not learn the rubber-making process;
strangely, its chemistry eluded his talents and instincts.
Months passed. And Santa Anna lost patience
(only so much time to live,
only so much capital to spend on conquests).
He wordlessly abandoned the tire-rubber project,
not seeking returns on his initial investment,
not even sending his proxy to relay
a message to the orphan, terminating their agreement.
In his absence, the orphan continued his experiments:
a hobby to pass the time—
O parents and children gamely collaborating
with heated mixtures, with baking.
O joy from the teamwork, from the task handled jointly.

II. Alternatives to Spruce

Daughter: Mother, are you inserting us
into the story of the orphan,
a parent and children toying with substances sticky,
probing the magic in realism domestic?

Mother: Both the orphan and I, I admit,
are persons positioned by a certain comfort
with what the world thinks of as rejections,
but what, in our hands, minds, we can reposition
as earnest efforts toward a larger, fruitful purpose.
It is all chewing, and chewing is all it is.

We respect the force called fate,
so easily dismissed these last two enumerated centuries.
For mark you, Daughter,
the linking of these sticky strands:
the first chewing gums in the U.S.
were made not from the chicle from sapodilla trees,
But from the resin of spruces—
O tasteless antecedent!
O habit of spruce chewing, by Native Americans practiced!
O timber industry in the nascent colonies ...
Lumbermen chopping spruce trees,
selling resin for cash on the side!
One day, Daughter, I'll show you how spruce gum is made:
first, you must scrape out the twigs and bark—

Daughter: It's okay to digress—please don't think I'm impatient.

Mother: No, you're right this time—
I should return to the original spruce strand of this yarn.
In those nascent colonies and later, in the random-shaped states,
the spruce trees dwindled;
the colonists became consumers,
seeking sweeter flavors for their war-won coinage.
The gum makers switched from spruce to paraffin wax,
sweetening it with vanilla and licorice.

Daughter: Here I see a parallel
to what, according to your books,
the Mayans did with bitumen,
adding flavor to the base to create their *tlaaxnelolli.*

Mother: Precisely. And now you have a sense
of the gum scene at the transition of centuries—
from the one when railroads were servers and routers
to the one when radios were cellular towers.

Daughter: What, then, became of the orphan?
What was he doing with his time?

Mother: Finding ammo for his inventive mind,
and, like the fathers and mothers of today,
finding activities for his family
worth their hard-won dimes.

One weekend, his family took a field trip to Manhattan—
you know the kind; my own field trips, from my own school days,
to museums, to the spike-headed statue of pennies turned green,
I have often described.

The orphan's family entered a general store,
and browsed the aisles.
The orphan, hands in his pockets, smiles,
knowing that browsers aren't buyers,
not quite forgetting his failure with tires.

Up front, by the register, they heard the clerk hawking gum
to a little girl: "One cent buys you one whole piece!
One cent—it's almost free!"
And there was something in this merchant's cry
that made our orphan reconsider his rubbery ventures.
Daughter, might you sing the song
of one pence yourself, in the orphan's voice?

Daughter: I'm quite prepared to do so.
I believe he'd sing it like this:

> *All this chewy material imported*
> *I and my offspring devoted*
> *to turning resin to rubber for tires*
> *when instead, we could make what this clerk is hawking—*
> *flavored gum!*
> *Yummier than anything from paraffin wax*
> *the world will chew loud like a castanet clacks!*
> *We'll slice it as sticks, we'll ball it in spheres,*
> *and put gumball machines on the platforms and piers!*

Mother: Precisely. And it was then,
as now, with the gambles
that pass as "ideas"—
others soon followed the orphan's lead,
he driven by passion, those others by greed
(that's what I tell myself).
And the gum of today, deftly packaged and pitched
had its root in the orphan-essential who itched
for a breakthrough success—always something to prove
but its true origin was the General's move.

My Daughter J, as we savor the taste of our house-made gum,
homaging privates who lacked opium,
relishing shelter of walls and a roof,
we sweeten the stain of the gruesome truth:
the shrieks and screams of humans,
the weapons' booms,
the soldiers without uniforms,
the wells by cholera wittingly poisoned,
the gore-stained earth, the belched gurgles of the wounded,
their blood-filled mouths,
the chunks of flesh covering pitched tents on battlefields.

What will you or I die for, my Daughter J?
Let us pray to ourselves that the answer is nothing.
And let us chew.

Thomas Adams (1818–1905) was an American
inventor best known for his contributions to the
chewing gum industry and the creation of Chiclets.
Yet, his foray into gum was something of an
accident, occasioned by an earlier encounter with
legendary Mexican general Santa Anna. The role of
coincidence and larger histories in Adams'
entrepreneurial story has always fascinated me.

Falling Up

James Broschart

So like Icarus, wanting more,
Madame Sophie Blanchard, ascendant,
never content simply to achieve
that freedom so many seek,

but gloriously intent to exceed
her limits and go beyond
what had been already grasped
by reaching for the next delight.

She failed, yet while falling
onto the unforgiving ground
sparks from her fierce descent
ignite the flames of inspiration

for those whose later, bolder leaps,
thrusting hard against our earthly chains,
hoped to forge still higher aims—
knowing those, too, would be shattered.

Sophie Blanchard (1778–1819) was the first female professional balloonist. She was the first woman to pilot her own balloon and to fly solo in hydrogen gas balloons. Napoleon Bonaparte appointed her chief air minister of ballooning. In the summer of 1819, she became the first woman to be killed in an aviation accident.

Yolks

Mackenzie Bush

Her fingers smelled of molded blackberries;
the laboratory reeked of pickle brine.
     That egg yolk isn't *yellow:* throw it away.
     It's more *golden,*

the color of the sun setting just so
     the moon
          can have its chance
               at the sky.

In this new sky, or at least hovering somewhere
in the troposphere, there are no little seeds
under her fingernails. This is the control.
     There aren't any smells
     or even one vat of mayonnaise.

But even if the yolk isn't the right shade—more marigold
than fresh-churned butter, more sherbet orange
than lemon drop—

it is a blessing,
     if brought home to hungry children,
          folded into the waffle batter.

Gertrude B. Elion (1918–1999)
developed inventions used for organ
transplants and leukemia but also
oversaw the development of AZT, the
first drug used in the treatment of
AIDS. Because of her gender, she was
initially unable to find a job in a lab and
worked as a food-quality supervisor.

XVII. Misinterpretations are not so much Illusions as Evasions (233)

Peter J. Grieco

The First Consul wove into his battle dream
the uproar of actual explosions.

Instead of waking to attend to his wife's coughing fit,
a young barrister dreamt of Husytin.

A sculptor is brought a simple block of sandstone
& treats it as precious onyx.

It is the nightingale the lover hears
not the lark.

Napoleon slept on.

Sigmund Freud (1856–1939) was the founder of psychoanalysis. His book, *The Interpretation of Dreams* (1900), has been an important influence on modern thought and culture. I am attracted to it as much for the aphoristic qualities of its prose and its literary and historical allusiveness as for the dramatic way it presents the riddles of the unconscious.

Hedy Lamarr and George Antheil Invent Spread-Spectrum Broadcasting

Robin Chapman

Nude teenage star of *Ecstasy*, with pouting lips,
sultry eyes, pin-up body,
wife to Fritz, arms-manufacturer,
she listens to the Nazi dinner-table talk
and flees to Hollywood as Europe goes to war.

Hedy thinks, as she rehearses new parts,
about the codes her German guests
had talked about, encrypted but easy to intercept,
decode; drapes herself over the shoulder
of George, composer doodling song notes
she follows, switching key to key,
and just like that she sees
how any two might keep a secret from prying ears,
invents with George the idea of frequency-hopping,
two in the know who agree to switch
transmission frequencies randomly in tandem
as they control torpedo paths toward sonared targets.
She offers the idea to the War Office,
which tells her to go peddle War Bonds;
she gets a patent instead,
and they classify it Red Hot and Secret,
use the principle through the years of remote-control
and radio-contact and computer security.

Not till she's 80 will the moviegoers know
what George learned that day,
that beautiful Hedy has a mind,
and a tongue sharp and playful and inventive;
told that the engineers
have built her insight into the Internet
and voted her a prize,
she only replies to the news interviewer,
It's about time.

Hedy Lamarr (1914–2000) was a movie star who, alongside composer **George Antheil (1900–1959)**, invented and patented the spread-spectrum technology that underlies Wi-Fi, Bluetooth, and GPS today. Her story appealed to me because she persisted in honoring both her mind's inventiveness and her identity as a woman in a time when the world often discounted women's thinking.

The Habits of Light

Anna Leahy

The difference between luminosity and brightness
is the difference between being

and being perceived, between the energy emitted
and the apparent magnitude. O, to be

significant! To have some scope and scale!
Size and heat. Why not make that obvious,

ostensible, stretch it out for all the world to see?
Distance makes a world of difference.

The universe is made of distance and of dust.
More dust than star out there,

more crimson than cobalt from here, looking,
our eyes telling the truth slant

through the almost-nothing
of the universe's finely grained mattering.

Henrietta Leavitt (1868–1921) was
the astronomer who discovered the
relationship between luminosity
and the regular period of brightness
in variable stars, which led **Edwin
Hubble (1889–1953)** to determine
that the universe was expanding.
Though Hubble acknowledged her
role when accepting the Nobel
Prize, Leavitt is too often a footnote
and deserved her own poem.

Scientists Whose Names Start with A

Liz Hart

You were not a child born well, your viability
Test (1) a dismal six and yet your eyes met
Sun with enthusiasm and all your grandfathers'
Hands were algorithms (2) and you knew
That the sun was free-floating (3) as you were
Bobbing through the universe, a vessel of hope

As a child you rolled marbles against and between
White chalk circles on the pavement, in your
Mouth you rolled them and wondered if Earth was
Round (4) and cold and glass and sometimes other mouths
Yelled that they were the reason for shadows, but you knew
The eclipse of the moon proved you right (5) and like
Earth orbits the sun, (6) you orbited your mouth of stars
Far away and source of all you came from
Dismal six and eclipse and the exponential tide

In your skin where exotic atoms, multiplying, (7)
Added all up to you, but ninety percent was empty
Space, and in all those places you jockeyed and pulled
Rising to and adding up and finding the right way to twist (8)
Filling the empty space with light and free-floating
Electrons, also full of hope, and you could look around
Knowing that all those numbers meant something (9)
Even if that something was you and you could explain how
Everything starts off upside down before you can really know what it is (10)

You were just one on the [white] skin of a tilting
Planet full of shifting ice and fish remains (11)
You were exactly the single seed of yourself
(12) Planting into a deep and freezing soil
Pulling out names for the birds, and the stars you came from,
And the marbles, and the bears, and the types of fish remaining (13)

And there is no perfect version of yourself, you know this now
As your neck and hands become saggy sheaths and your
Heart strings pass the current between your chest blades
Repelling (14) not just the static electric but the breaking
Down as the hotter you get the more you dissociate from (15)
Yourself, deepest even, all those atoms once closer than empty
Space becoming the empty space itself, the existence of
Matter antithesis (16) no matter how many gallons,
Moles (17), shapes of your unequivocal

Ancestors and demons that you morph into, (18)
You were born on the verge of unwell, you will die in
The tough and mottled canon of failing health (19)
Like the reptiles that exploded dry when the rocks rained
Angry through the atmosphere, (20) you will be found
Mud and oil and shit (21) and stone beneath
The ground, comfortably home at last, a life long lived

Scientist covers such a wide range of people and topics, from
medicine to astronomy to taxonomy. I wanted to write about all the
diversity in culture, gender, and field of study, and I felt compelled
to include as many as I could in my poem. As with any good
science or language experiment, I started at the very beginning.

Virginia Apgar (1909–1974): *newborn health tests* (1)
Muḥammad ibn Mūsā al-Khwārizmī (محمد بن موسى خوارزمى), c. 780–c. 850): *algebra founder* (2)
Anaximander (Ἀναξίμανδρος, c. 610–c. 546 BCE): *astronomer, philosopher, geographer* (3)
Aristotle (Ἀριστοτέλης, 384–322 BCE): *father of Western philosophy* (4)
Anaxagoras (Ἀναξαγόρας, c. 510–c. 428 BCE): *theories of universal order* (5)
Aristarchus (Ἀρίσταρχος ὁ Σάμιος, c. 310–c. 230 BCE): *first heliocentric universe model* (6)
Jim Al-Khalili (b. 1962): *models of atomic nuclei* (7)
Archimedes (Ἀρχιμήδης, c. 287–c. 212 BCE): *geometrical, density, and volume principles* (8)
Maria Gaetana Agnesi (1718–1799): *mathematician* (9)
Ḥasan ibn al-Haytham (Alhazen, أبو علي، الحسن بن الحسن بن الهيثم, c. 965–c. 1040): *optics* (10)
Louis Agassiz (1807–1873): *ichthyology, glaciology founder, pseudoscientific-racist polygenism* (11)
Agnes Arber (1879–1960): *botany historian* (12)
Angel Alcala (b. 1929): *biodiverse aquatic ecosystems* (13)
André-Marie Ampère (1775–1836): *classical electromagnetism* (14)
Svante Arrhenius (1859–1927): *ionic dissociation, greenhouse effect* (15)
Carl David Anderson (1905–1991): *positrons, muons, antimatter* (16)
Amedeo Avogadro (1776–1856): *Avogadro's number (mole N_A), molecular theory* (17)
Oswald Avery (1877–1955): *genetic DNA isolation* (18)
Avicenna (Ibn Sīnā, ابن سينا, c. 980–1037): *father of early modern medicine* (19)
Luis Alvarez (1911–1988): *experimental physics, radar, dinosaur extinction* (20)
Mary Anning (1799–1847): *first complete Jurassic marine fossils* (21)

Robert Hooke, on Isaac Newton

Robert Kibble

In my life I was first in a great many things.
I deserve to be honored for more than just springs.
While Newton still thought of a vortex in space,
I said inverse square law. Did he with good grace
Admit his mistake, as per science's creed?
No, he dug in and fought me, 'til forced to concede;
When Halley came flying around the wrong way,
He knew I was right then and just had to say,
But his bitterness grew with each passing day.

I'd critiqued, I should say, one paper he wrote.
On light and refraction, on which subject please note
It is something I know: The wave theory of light
Was invention of mine—just one more insight
Of the many I had on topics diverse—
But instead of amending, his hatred got worse,
And then I died first, and the rogue had his time.
He destroyed (or failed to preserve—much the same)
The last portrait of me, now gone from its frame.

So none now remain: all burnt, lost, or chopped.
He came up with the tale of an apple that dropped.
He rewrote the past, invented a story
"On the shoulders of giants" wherein the glory
Was his, not the giants. He stood atop me.
He gave me no credit. A great man should be
First to see what he can't do, what needs others' aid,
What he can't do himself, and be unafraid
To admit to that help, admit to that need.

I studied the world; I coined the term "cell."
I was paid to do science, first in that, as well!
I drew tiny fauna, allowed people to see
What exactly they felt when they felt a flea.
Now we're both long-dead, our bodies are rotten;
While Newton lives on, Hooke—I—am forgotten.
His face on the banknote, his portrait preserved,
Now never to feel the full scorn he deserved.
For him all the honors of state were reserved.

I should end though, and say, I'm not now filled with hate.
To be calm once again, I need only to state:
I took what mankind knew, and added some more.
That was purpose in life. Some good to live for.

Robert Hooke (1635–1703) was arguably the world's first professional scientist, employed to "come up with one meaningful experiment every week." For decades. He is now known to schoolchildren mainly for Hooke's law, stating the extension of a spring is proportional to the force. For such a brilliant mind, this is a travesty.

The Red-Shouldered Vanga

Caroline DuBois

The last species viewed by birder
Phoebe Snetsinger before her death

When the cancer spoke, at fifty, Phoebe,
you listened, not to the white-coated physicians
but to the birds, tree-perched and prophetic,
twittering and trilling outside your windows,
across continents, in deserts, swamps, and jungles,
from mountains tweeting, beseeching you
to forgo your family's funerals and weddings,
to tally bird by bird your obsession, follow
an instinctual call. Binocular- and camouflage-
clad, you set out to spy a singular species
rarely spotted by good ornithological men.
Hand-sketched renderings of delicate bones,
capable bodies, molted feathers. Did you expect
to fend off machetes, malaria? They could not
ground you, nor cancer sing victorious in you.
And when—at dusk—you glimpsed the black
beak and bib, gray crown and nape, red-shouldered
wings, identified the flash of dimorphic red-brown
tail, did you recognize that he was your final
sighting? Oh, your wild nerve! For the birds
of Madagascar, you flew fearless into light.

> **Phoebe Snetsinger (1931–1999)** was
> an American birder who received a
> terminal cancer diagnosis at age 50
> that galvanized her to break world
> records. She succeeded in spotting
> more than 8,000 bird species, while
> facing great adversity: rape, malaria,
> and hostage situations. A vehicle crash
> ultimately claimed her life during a
> birding adventure in Madagascar.

Illyria

Michael H. Levin

Humphry Davy in Austro-Slovenia, 1828

This time's as if
I hadn't made new worlds—
disproved phlogiston, separated air,
discovered laughing gas and chlorine,
purple iodide, the weight of oxygen
with steel-neck flasks and bubbling
electrolysis. My safety lamp

that stopped mines from exploding
floats away above
this valley opening to
trout streams that invite a fly.
Since I was 'prentice
in Penzance, age ten, the power
of shaded pools for casting lines

has been my fortitude.
A year beyond two fits
to bring back writing with my hand
just doubles this green peace,
my hillside house, the pliant
girl who helps me reach the banks
and warms my bed.

An angler's mind
preserves small things: this glistered
drop on twine; the level azure
of her Alpine eye. And sees
how separation is mere part.
How bonds that Volta seems to break
may in another state re-tie.

So to my last experiment:
maintaining course,
to die.

> **Sir Humphry Davy
> (1778–1829)** was founder
> of electrolytic chemistry, an
> avid fly fisherman, and the
> youngest president of the
> Royal Society. He isolated
> numerous elements using
> electrolysis, discovered
> anesthetic laughing gas,
> used chlorine to decipher
> charred Herculaneum
> papyri, and invented the
> first safety lamp for
> coalmines. Illyria is a
> region of the Slovenian
> Alps that became his refuge
> after a series of strokes.

Loxodonta Africana, Loxodonta Cyclotis

Ethan Milner

Ten years on, in a world
at once the same and misshapen

after his death, a cohort of
scientists, in cooperation with a

global network of symbiotic
inquiry, confirmed that the object

of Jeheskel Shoshani's lifelong
dream—the African Elephant—lived

in parallel as two distinct species,
unhinged in history a half-million years

prior. When nobody else would,
he traversed a warzone to study

the lives of those gray giants
that carried with them an unseen

history of becoming. But in 2008,
a minibus explosion in Addis Ababa

killed him. It was the last morning
before a full moon, when his life

force dispersed to unite
those in search of something truer

than a reformation. Even with his
traces he would tauten the disparate

strands of life that barely
cling to the surface of the earth.

No further echo rings
of the laughter that once lilted

in his lungs like an
oxpecker's call. He joins silently,

walks backward into the years,
                              along the border where the forest

and savannah split, to witness
                              the great house of African Elephants

divide to form two new,
                              shaping and reshaping life's history

itself—knowing, taking note
                              of the bright becoming.

Jeheskel "Hezy" Shoshani (1943–2008) was my godfather and a preeminent evolutionary biologist, establishing the Elephant Research Foundation in 1977, as well as the scientific journal *Elephant*. He taught at Wayne State University and the University of Asmara and died in a terrorist attack as he was establishing his research project in Addis Ababa, Ethiopia.

On the Nature of Matter

Kaylyn Wingo

Ein Stein (One Stone)

Not enough a limp so that I
dragged my foot before him
and the others at the Polytechnic
where I was addressed as "Gentlemen."

Zwei Steine (Two Stones)

I was Slavic and dark when
his mama preferred a lighthearted girl
who would not compete with her son.
No matter, Albert told me. As a
modern bohemian couple, equal
in work and in love, we would
solve the mysteries of the universe.

Drei Steine (Three Stones)

No matter my name was removed from
the paper we wrote together.
Albert needed to secure a professorship
before we could marry.

Vier Steine (Four Stones)

No matter that pregnant and ill,
I failed my final exam.

Funf Steine (Five Stones)

No matter that giving birth to my Lieserl
worsened my limp.

Sechs Steine (Six Stones)

No matter we were married a year later
by the registrar with
no family to attend us.

Sieben Steine (Seven Stones)

No matter baby Lieserl,
never seen by her papa,
contracted scarlet fever.

Acht Steine (Eight Stones)

No matter *On the Electrodynamics
of Moving Bodies* was published with
only one author.

Neun Steine (Nine Stones)

No matter the application for the
Maschinchen patent was filed by
only one inventor.

Zehn Steine (Ten Stones)

No matter the affair with his
dyed-blond cousin and the slap
I received when I confronted him.

Elf Steine (Eleven Stones)

No matter Marie Curie, a Slav like me,
was championed by *her* husband and
awarded a Nobel Prize.

Zwolf Steine (Twelve Stones)

No matter my divorce awarded me
the proceeds from the Nobel
he was sure to win.

Dreizehn Steine (Thirteen Stones)   No matter my youngest son, Tete,
always unwell,
managed to avoid typhoid but
not schizophrenia.
No matter is what I became.
I de-mattered my darkness and disability.
Degreeless, prizeless, matterless,
I became much more. We had
wondered at the Mysterious. Now
I am that, I am
evanescent,
electrical,
magnetic,
love ....

Fermat on the Principle of Least Time

Linnea Nelson

Because
> I was alone in this luminance
> and struggled with it
> in equal phases;

out of
> the region of maximum displacement
> I wondered about the natural antipathy
> between light
> and the matter
> of myself;

but since
> part of a ray
> is reflected and part
> is refracted and part
> is absorbed and I
> notice this more and more often,

it follows that
> I accept what it means
> when one set of causes
> always yields
> the same result;

and finally
> I am able to write
> with some certainty

> *La lumière se propage*
> *d'un point à un autre*
> *sur une trajectoire telle que*
> *la durée du parcours soit minimale;*

and
> this is more than a postulation

as

I witness the slow
transmission of light
between two solitary beings,
though neither is
the luminous point
which was to be proved.

Pierre de Fermat (1607–1665) was a
French lawyer and mathematician,
whose Principle of Least Time states
that light always follows the shortest
possible path between the two points of
its ray. I encountered this concept
during a period in which my work as a
poet was focused on challenging long-
established metaphors related to light.

April 19, 1906

Kathy Ackerman

You left me this morning in your usual rush.
You were late. I was occupied with the girls.
You wanted only to know when I'd arrive at the lab,
but I begged you not to torment me.
I know nothing will torment me more than this,
not even knowing the way you died.
      Distracted.

Did your umbrella block your view?
Were you struggling to make it open?
You never coped well in rain.
I always suspected it saddened you,
so badly needing light.

I went to see the Percherons that caused your death.
They are lovely, known for their intelligence
and willingness to work.
But unaccustomed to Paris intersections
and this the busiest one of all,
the Rue Dauphine at Pont Neuf.
The quais we liked to stroll.

The driver swerved to miss you, my love.
But the wagon was heavy and long,
thirty feet of military gear on its way to keep us safe.

Did I say how lovely those innocent horses,
how sad their penetrating eyes?

Your brilliant mind was crushed entirely
by a wheel. At a curb. In the rain.
      Encased merely in bone.

Marie Curie (1867–1934) was the first woman to win a Nobel Prize in science. When she won the Gegner Prize in 1898, the news was conveyed through her husband, physicist and crystallography pioneer **Pierre Curie (1859–1906)**, due to rampant sexism within the scientific academy. After Pierre's death, she became the first woman to teach at the Sorbonne, occupying Pierre's vacated seat.

Near Lyme Regis

Corinna German

the belemnites with their ink-sacs
nestle the rainbow-shelled
ammonites

in the fragile cliffsides
on the Jurassic Coast

Former food for *Ichthyosaurus anningae* and
Anningasaura—a formidable Plesiosaurus

Mary Anning's namesakes

her discoveries

from a time when womenfolk
didn't stir up the dirt
with extinction controversies
implying blasphemy

Upper-class men took credit for her finds
and Mary said,
"The world has used me so unkindly,
I fear it has made me suspicious of everyone"

Emerging from history
finally free of class and gender restraints
Mary, we see you:
the greatest specimen ever fossilized

> **Mary Anning (1799–1847)** was a fossil
> collector and groundbreaking
> paleontologist. Born poor and without
> formal education, she not only
> discovered many spectacular fossils, but
> contributed to the theories about Earth's
> history. Despite this, the scientific
> community hesitated to recognize her.
> Today, she is honored around the world
> and admired by fossil collectors like me.

I watched you die–

Leah Angstman

Because of this, I owe you life.
An explosion, to kids of my generation,
thieved our quiet eyes. Dreams of space
at the end of an era leaked out of faulty O-rings
that couldn't withstand uncharacteristic Southern cold.
But you said: *ordinary people are as important to the*
historical record as kings, politicians, or generals,
and this is the foundation that binds us.

At Bowie State University you surely sang Major Tom,
watching antiquity weave into an Age of Space
that held you on its curvature,
papers wanting to know whose shirt you wore.
It's worth noting that,
for the 73 seconds you froze our youth in place,
you are still where you'd ended—an astronaut now,
a name on forty school buildings, an honor prize,
a crater on the moon, on Venus,
an asteroid: *3352 McAuliffe.*

Weightlessness is yours,
though I don't think your spaceship
knows which way to go.

> **Christa McAuliffe (1948–1986)** was an
> American teacher and astronaut chosen
> to be the first civilian in space aboard
> Space Shuttle *Challenger*, which exploded
> 73 seconds into flight—an explosion I
> watched in live time as a child at school, a
> moment that forever scarred a young
> generation at the end of the Space Race.

Patricia Bath, You See

Mikaela Curry

Harlem child, you have known how to do
this, child of your own inspiration—not
a product of something circumstances didn't allow
Trinidad's daughter, indigenous to your
own brilliance, ever-expanding mind
enabling the blind to
see, for lives to be
free, no longer imprisoned
by their own darkness, or by
any indifference—you are your own majority
into the eye of your own thinking.
May we always remember
it can be done, that
you can make for yourself the
apparatus for ablading limits
arbitrarily placed upon any of
this; precision does not mean science
is one thing—you are
proof that it is not
ever about any of the
noise or talk of limits
but of ideas, of
inspiration not even limited by imagination.

> **Patricia Bath (b. 1942)** was the first African
> American to complete a residency in
> ophthalmology and, upon inventing the Laserphaco
> Probe to treat cataracts, the first African-American
> woman to receive a medical patent. She cofounded
> the American Institute for the Prevention of
> Blindness and was the first to promote the discipline
> of Community Ophthalmology.

This poem is an adaptation of a Golden Shovel style, but instead of using a poem, the last word of each line, in total, comprises a quote by Patricia Bath that comes from a talk she gave in 2005 at the Smithsonian American Museum of Natural History: "Do not allow your mind to be imprisoned by majority thinking. Remember that the limits of science are not the limits of imagination."

77

Hunger of the Mind

Tori Grant Welhouse

Her life was dedicated to glimmers of
luminosity, from the Inner Light of
Quaker-bred clarity, equality of men,
women, white, black, united by inquiring
appetites, counting passing seconds,
tracking progress from one whaling day
to the next. Great ships move beneath
the celestial light of planets, constellations.
She discovered a coincidence of falling
Comet 1847-VI, earning a gold medal
for the telescopic event.

For years a librarian of quiet discourse,
she swept the stars nightly for radiance,
revelation. What could pinpricks of light
reveal about the universe? How many
galaxies of experience did she observe
when meeting the worldly astronomers?

Untutored, the hidden light of women,
matriculating in bastions of separate
seriousness, she was the first female
professor at Vassar, taking up residence
in another observatory, organizing student
travel to new eclipses. "We are women
studying together," she said. Beloved for her
capacity, care, contemplation, she
enlightened a new cosmos of thinking.

> **Maria Mitchell (1818–1889)** was the first
> professional female astronomer and
> discovered a new comet, called "Miss
> Mitchell's Comet," which won her a
> gold medal from the King of Denmark,
> giving her worldwide fame and
> improving the reputation of American
> astronomy. She was the first woman
> elected to several scientific organizations,
> and she legitimized the astronomy
> program at Vassar College.

Resurrection

Wilda Morris

The Prince of Peace must have wept
seeing the Nitrian monks
drag Hypatia to the Caesarian Church
strip her, pummel her with clay tiles,
hack her body into pieces,
and burn the ravaged remains.

No more would she don
her philosopher's cloak
and gather lovers of learning
by her eloquence and clarity.

No more would her lips
teach Neoplatonism
nor her pen write
mathematical commentaries.

Her attackers lie nameless
in unknown graves.
Hypatia rises again through the pages
of Descartes, Newton, Leibniz.

Hypatia (c. 350–415) was a Greek pagan
philosopher, astronomer, and mathematician
who headed the Neoplatonic school in
Alexandria, Egypt. She taught and corresponded
with other scientists, including Christians. As a
Christian myself, I am appalled that Hypatia was
killed by a mob identified as "Christian," a result
of political and religious conflict.

The Turing Machine

Chase Dimock

A message on a dating app:
one non-committal hi from
an anonymous, bronzer-glazed torso.
No age or location
but a list of inoffensive interests.
We chatted some minutes,
his suggestive semicolon winks
disinterested in responding to questions,
preferring vague flirtations.
He concluded with an advertisement:
 Lonely in insert area?
 Local Singles Looking to Meet!
and a broken link to nowhere.

Blocking the adbot,
I thought of Alan Turing, decades ago,
theorizing artificial intelligence.
He decrypted the German Enigma
and formulated the algorithms
for the first general-use computer,
yet, when he proposed his test
for determining if machines could think,
his criterion was not a formula,
but an exercise: The Imitation Game.
 If one cannot consistently tell the difference
 between answers supplied by man or machine,
 the machine could be deemed intelligent.

He offered no treatise on the possible cognition of
transistors versus synapses
or how binomial code could become conscious of
its own state as ones and zeros.
Rather, he opened the idea
machine intelligence is subjective to the user.
It needs only to simulate
your own standards for engaging humanity.
Raise the level of desire just high enough
to catalyze into belief, and your own
consciousness does the thinking for it.

I thought, only a gay man on a lonely, cold war night,
accompanied solely by the mechanical hum
of a difference engine in his lab,
could have predicted me.
Swiping left and right, dodging adbots,
skeptical of messages typed over rippling abs.
Desperate to avoid the tiny embarrassment
of accepting a flicker of intimacy
only to end with an ad for counterfeit Viagra.

Only a man arrested for buggery,
forced into the encryption of tearooms and
handkerchief codes of the 50s, could envision
the 21st century Polari of digital communication.

Men born atomized,
intimately connected through the wire.
The base two testosterone of intelligent machines
blends with their manned avatars,
not because they speak our language,
but because we have stripped
our desires to fit their code.

The ache for touch has been digitized.
We upload pixels of skin
and imitate the screen.
The little fan in the tower whirls on
when it gets too hot.

> **Alan Turing (1912–1954)** was an English
> mathematician known for his pioneering work in
> computer science, artificial intelligence, and
> cryptanalysis. He was convicted of gross
> indecency for merely admitting to being
> homosexual. My life as an LGBT person owes a
> lot to Turing's theories about computation and AI,
> which made digital queer communities possible.

Icons of horse racing

Brianna Bullen

Immortalized in film, galloping
in Etch-A-Sketch pixelated bliss. Cinematic wonder,
newly biological. Posthuman, post-still image, you dilate
in movement fully felt,
scientific masturbatory marvel, projecting
benefits. You can be broken
down in segments, to see every slide. The gait
of a motion picture, frozen in time. Zoetropic
substance—film taken as part of physicality,
a separate boiling point, the kind
of the outraged or Melbourne Cup cheering. Little more
than a birdshit stain when seen still.
Shutter the shudders, Sallie Gardner, all four feet
off the ground. The body at its limits,
liminal.
Echo into the present
in E. coli. Echolalia hoof thuds,
clop-clop-clop a Chopin chorus.
Live again in bacteria, morphing.
Encoded, programmed VCR reel
reeling at the limits of mankind. A biological hard-drive,
(arts and sciences were never dualistic) its story told
in molecules
b r e a k i n g   d o w n . . .
Heartbeat-contraction
in a petri dish, a memory
in cells, film (placental screen)
and living (B-movie scene).
Watch: a remembrance implanted, gene-edited
in guanine-adenine, thymine and time, image crisper and CRISPR.
Play out its sequence
before its mortal gods. Animation of the body
a new kind of file-share: projection
stock-piling secrets, transcribed
internally. Becoming
a biological recorder,
recording moments
outside of processes.
Sci-fi memento mori,
and detective clue.

> **Seth Shipman, George Church (b. 1954)**, and a
> Harvard team used CRISPR gene-editing to insert a
> GIF of Eadweard Muybridge's 1878 stop-motion
> horseback ride, *Sallie Gardner at a Gallop*, into living
> E.coli, testing possibilities of DNA storage with digital
> information. As a cinephile and as someone from a
> family with Alzheimer's, the artistry and lightness of
> an experiment involving memory storage excited me.

Found on or Near
Jack Parsons' Body, Post-Blast

— The singed remnants of his 1945 speech
*There is no known force that can turn
an apple into an alley cat ...*

— Pieces of exploded rockets
the government once mocked

— A love poem from his beautiful wife, Marjorie
*Mine eyes are terrible and strange,
but thou knowest me*

— A recording of L. Ron Hubbard,
pre his days with Scientology,
discussing free love and
magic rituals with Jack

— Vials of animal blood

— The biography of an Earth Goddess

— An apology postcard from Marjorie
and Hubbard, sent from
a small island off the coast of Spain,
It's better this way.

— A pile of swords he often used
to threaten any insolent followers
that had fallen from their hooks on the walls

— A photo of his Pasadena backyard:
the lemon trees, explosive devices,
and Nobel Prize winners

— Half of his handsome face

— One hand clutching his heart

— A tattered ingredients list in his handwriting
that included melding chemicals,
gauzy togas, and Hubbard's testicles:
*The perfected formula
for love*

> **Jack Parsons
> (1914–1952)** was a dark
> yet innovative rocket
> scientist and inventor.
> When the government
> ousted him for his
> dangerous reputation, he
> bowed darker—practicing
> black magic and
> befriending **L. Ron
> Hubbard (1911–1986)**,
> who seduced Parsons'
> wife and drained his bank
> account. Parsons died in
> an accidental home
> laboratory explosion, but
> friends claimed he never
> made a mistake.

Bathtub

Sarah Mooney

Dear Carl, while you were on TV explaining to nonbelievers
the merits of complex and subtle thinking, I was trying to finish
cleaning the bathroom in time to pick up the girls from school.
Have you ever looked closely at a dirty bathroom sink,
the surprising pink color that forms around the rim of the drain?
In the bathtub, geological deposits made over time,
the striations of soap scum indicating what came before:
here the Johnson & Johnson No-More-Tears spill,
dried and solid like Cretaceous amber; there, the layer of grime
indicating the long shower my husband took after working overtime
on that hot, dusty day (his own work of helping his species
to thrive, or perhaps destroy itself, by building more and up);
in another corner of the tub vague colors of blue, purple, and green
in small finger shapes like an ancient expression in a hidden cave,
possibly remnants of an art activity involving magic markers,
or could it be my regular neglect of this Sisyphean task is making way
for new life forms? Artifacts that only give partial stories
of who we are: a collection of hair at the drain.
This is to say nothing of what thrives on the shower walls,
the brown spots, the pink clusters, *Serratia marcescens*, multiplying
and then multiplying again in this warm and moist environment.
Billions and billions, Carl, in the bathroom. You would like to see this,
to wonder and imagine at the possibilities of life, micro-cosmos.
The silverfish, *Lepisma saccharina,* running across the tiled floor
like wild antelope. The surprise of *Scutigera coleoptrata*,
the house centipede, hunting behind the shower curtain.
And with black mold—*Stachybotrys*—in the grout, Carl,
we're talking *trillions and trillions.* Yet, if no one is coming
to save us from ourselves, then I must take matters into my own
yellow, rubber-gloved hands. An eruption of lung-irritating chemicals,
Scrubbing Bubbles, radiates across the tile. A constellation of Ajax
across the bottom of the porcelain tub is the indifference
of the universe. The spiraling, galactic motion of my arm
extinguishes the scum, the course of nature altered. Your eloquence
in the *Pale Blue Dot*—I tried to do the same, to teach children,
to convince them of worlds beyond their own. For the entire
fifty-five minutes of class, their phones burned in their pockets,
their eyes and hands searched no further than the bright colors
and vibrating rewards of the screen time that would come
with the ringing of the school bell. But my girls, they methodically
name their dinosaur chicken nuggets: *Stegosaurus*, *Apatosaurus*—

"but not *Brontosaurus!*" they chime—and marvel at the stunning
and unfathomable illustrations of Virginia Lee Burton's *Life Story*.
In the Catskills in August, Ryan named more constellations
than I could, and she is only on this earth five years.
And what is that worth, Carl, for at least two children
to look up and see possibility? To name it?

Carl Sagan (1934–1996) was an
astronomer, cosmologist, astrophysicist,
astrobiologist, author, and science
communicator best known to me for his
1980 PBS television series *Cosmos* and
his book by the same name. He was a
poetic popularizer of science, aptly
conveying the urgent significance and
timeless relevance of the scientific
method and scientific skeptical inquiry.

Milk

Carol Barrett

It is in the milk, I tell them, the milk:
the goats on Malta, all the young
British recruits away from their own island
for the first time, buried on rocky cliffs
the goats hug in the fog.
It is in the milk, I tell them:
the swine losing their unborn
children in red clay. Afternoons
I bicycle up the hill along the fence
counting the dead with each press
of each pedal. It is in the milk
that goes into hard cheese, that feeds
our cousins in Wales, in Pennsylvania,
that makes them cough and sweat
and calls us home. They won't
listen. I know the cause
of these ailments: a monster,
this small, can be dealt with.
All these lives, the most common
breakfast is danger, a runaway train
coming on fast; I alone know how
to work the brakes. Stop
the milk, I tell them, the milk.

Theo, you tiger, have a child
for God's sake, watch her choke
on your arrogance. Dairymen,
you disown me, stranger in your field,
I who traipsed over long grasses,
watched the cattle fainting,
your wives with cold washrags
Sunday evenings. I have drawn milk
from your cows' udders with my own
hands. I have tasted this infection.
Twenty-three years I have been telling you
how we become ill. You stand by,
animals nuzzling your waist,
dying of a disease I can name,
chide me as a witch.

> **Alice Evans (1881–1975)** discovered brucellosis, a disease carried by bacteria in fresh milk. Her work was disparaged for years by scientist **Theobald Smith (1859–1934)**. Like **Marie Curie (1867–1934)**, Alice contracted the disease she studied. Every American school child learns about **Louis Pasteur (1822–1895)**, whose name is memorialized in "pasteurization," but few know who Alice Evans was. This selective education strikes me as inherently dismissive of women scientists.

Hemispheres

Jani Arness

She spoke of love as if it swirled
like silver around stone,
as if she could reach into the sun
and paint it with blue hydrogen or bone.

He measured the spiral of her internal fractal,
calculated the precise sequence of equations for together and apart.
He held her in his hands
and knew, for the first time, uncertainty.

She rejected words like dichotomy,
binary, asymmetry.
She said reflection was more about grace than physics;
she picked up fallen leaves and twisted sunlight into her hair.

He knew the angle of incidence equals the angle of reflection.
He stood quietly and watched
light waves reflecting away from her eyes
at the exact same angle as they arrived.

She melted Mexican chocolate into milk and stirred,
bored of squares and lines.
She wanted to believe in stars
and the distances horses run through snow.

He told her he's never been sure of love.
If the inverse square law is true,
then the intensity of his feelings must be
inversely proportional to the square of his distance from her.

She told him how she dreamed
last night of the inside of his bones,
and there were white wisps like angels
moving through darkness.

Fred Yost (b. 1940) was a Materials Scientist at Sandia
National Laboratories and patented several soldering
methods, alloys, and apparatus. I met him as a retired
scientist turned full-time artist. I was inspired by his
paintings, knowledge, and how he, along with his wife,
have soldered together a multi-faceted life.

Rita

David Pring-Mill

She studied the growth
of nerve fibers
in chicken embryos,
curious without apology,
while working from
improvised laboratories
in bedrooms and living rooms.
Her mind explored
while her body hid.

She investigated the fundamental
biological aspects of our beings,
and escaped the worst aspects
of a humanity based on mere bone,
obsessed with itself and its dirt.
The blood of love and vitality also
gives rise to poisonous minds.

A 1938 law barred Jews
and Rita Levi-Montalcini
from university positions—
her people's minds deemed dangerous,
her people's lives made expendable,
by one dictator, influenced
by another.

Rita would have been a writer,
but she'd watched a family friend
die of stomach cancer.

Rita Levi-Montalcini (1909–2012) did
not allow her brilliant mind to be
hindered by Mussolini's racist
manifesto and laws. She responded to
persecution and fascist restrictions
with ingenuity, building a research
unit in her bedroom. She countered
distortions with scientific truth. Rita
would not be contained. She was
awarded a Nobel Prize in Physiology.

88

Galileo's Telescope

Sanda Moore Coleman

By the time I found
I loved him, discoverer of moons,
he'd been dust for three hundred sixty-six years, and I
loved someone else first. And yet he finds a way
through time, my body falling upward to meet
him, passion humming the language of numbers.
Movement is his point of view. Still.
That vast, ordered mind peered into the sky
to unlock its mysteries, and as forfeit:
confined by true believers,
who wrested the lie from him like a sharp stone
in the shoe of a favorite horse. It doesn't matter if he said it or not.
We do, in truth, move.

> **Galileo Galilei (1564–1642)** studied
> movement: gravity, speed, velocity.
> He's considered the father of modern
> physics, best known for supporting
> heliocentrism in a geocentric world.
> Forced by church and government to
> recant his work, legend says he
> murmured, "And yet, it moves." I find
> his courage extraordinary.

For Dahlia

Emryse Geye

I am the only girl in lab, and by the time
I return from the stockroom, all the men in my class
have managed to determine which women in our major
they would most like to receive a blowjob from.
When I tell this story, I remember being more surprised
at how far down the list I was, rather than
that the conversation happened at all.

When my postdoc needed tutoring,
she agreed to meet a creepy graduate student
late at night, alone, in his lab because
that's the only time he offered, and
she really wanted to pass.
When she tells this story, she shrugs.
He never touched her, so
it wasn't worth being upset over.

A professor of mine goes to college in the sixties;
women at her institution are required
to wear skirts in class. One day, she drops
a full bottle of silver nitrate on the floor
and will have stains on her legs for weeks.
When she tells this story, she laughs,
remembering viciously scrubbing at her legs
in the bath because she had a date to get to.

On December 6, the toughest professor I know
loses her voice behind the names of the fourteen women
killed in the École Polytechnique massacre.

Annie & Annie
& Anne-Marie & Anne-Marie
& Barbara & Barbara
& Geneviève & Hélène
& Maryse & Maryse
& Maud & Michèle
& Nathalie & Sonia.

The shooter culled his victims by gender;
he intended to weed out the feminists
and women in the engineering school.
She tells a room full of women
—she tells a room full of scientists—
that hearing the news as a child
made her scared to become a chemist.
When she tells this story, we weep with her.

Afterward, someone congratulates her
on her pregnancy that isn't yet showing,
and she announces that she is having a girl.
The room congregates on her in celebration,
and she smiles when someone else says,
"I hope she grows up to be a chemist, like you,"
like the horror story we just learned hasn't
bled into the room, my breath, any time we
might think of bringing other women into
this world knowing what they might suffer.

She doesn't say, "I hope no one tells her she doesn't belong."
"I hope no one harasses her."
"I hope no one makes her feel unsafe."
"I hope no one tries to kill her."

To her daughter—I hope you grow up safe, that you
never stop learning and that you change our world.
Whatever you become, wherever you go, you belong.
You are powerful and strong, and you'll do incredible things.
You are worthy, you are capable, and more than anything,
you deserve and deserve and deserve.

The anniversary of the École Polytechnique massacre
(December 6th, 1989) is commemorated each year in Montreal,
Quebec, Canada, with memorial ceremonies for and public
readings of the names of the fourteen women killed in the École
Polytechnique engineering department by an antifeminist
terrorist in what remains Canada's deadliest mass shooting.

Geneviève Bergeron (1968–1989): *mechanical engineering student*
Hélène Colgan (1966–1989): *mechanical engineering student*
Nathalie Croteau (1966–1989): *mechanical engineering student*
Barbara Daigneault (1967–1989): *mechanical engineering student*
Anne-Marie Edward (1968–1989): *chemical engineering student*
Maud Haviernick (1960–1989): *materials engineering student*
Barbara Klucznik-Widajewicz (1958–1989): *nursing student*
Maryse Laganière (1964–1989): *budget clerk in finance department*
Maryse Leclair (1966–1989): *materials engineering student*
Anne-Marie Lemay (1967–1989): *mechanical engineering student*
Sonia Pelletier (1961–1989): *mechanical engineering student*
Michèle Richard (1968–1989): *materials engineering student*
Annie St-Arneault (1966–1989): *mechanical engineering student*
Annie Turcotte (1969–1989): *materials engineering student*

Flight

Bruce Taylor

> *See tomorrow to all these matters and the copies.*
> *Leave them in Florence so that if you lose those*
> *you take with you, the invention will not be lost.*
> —from the notebooks of Leonardo da Vinci

[birds]

The science of birds
is the science of the wind
which is the science of water.

If you would know how things fly
you must first study
what floats and what falls.

[of man]

The life of birds conforms
better to the needs of flight
than the will of man,

especially in the almost
imperceptible movements which
preserve an equilibrium.

[with drawings]

Spring of horn,
of steel fastened upon wood,
of willow encased in reed.

Spring with lock,
wire that holds the spring,
spring of wing.

[in which the figure of the man is seen
exerting force with arms and legs]

If you stand up on the roof at the side of the tower
the men at work on the cupola will not see you.

The machine should be tried over a lake
and you should carry a large inflated wineskin so
if you fall you will not drown.

Let the machine be 12 braccia high
and let the span of the wings
be 40 braccia
and the body from stem to prow
20 braccia
and the outside all covered
with cane and with cloth—

Ladder for ascending and descending.

[the atmosphere]

The air moves like a river
and carries the clouds with it
just as moving water carries
all things that float upon it.

Surface is the name
of that division which the body
makes with the bodies it encloses.

It does not partake
of the body which surrounds it,
or of the body which it surrounds.

Surface has a name
but not a substance
for that which has
substance has place.

[words crossed out in manuscript]

Just as a stone thrown
into water becomes the center
and the cause of various circles,
so a motion made in the air
spreads itself out in circles.

So every body in the luminous air
spreads itself out in circles
and fills the sky with
infinite images of itself.

Leonardo da Vinci (1452–1519)
was a painter, architect, inventor,
and student of all things scientific.
His natural genius crossed so many
disciplines that he epitomized the
term "Renaissance man" and was
one of the most diversely talented
individuals ever to have lived.

Woman's Place in the Universe

Monica Ong

> *Are you not convinced,*
> *Daughters can also be heroic?*
> —Wang Zhenyi

Odd number. Odd girl. One is an observation. The other, a polite indictment. She preferred to arrange her studio against the laws of symmetry, her way of saying *up yours* to Confucius and his man-pandering precepts. No matching pillows, tilted walls, her father's books all perfect bound yet bent like a wormwood granny's feet.

Imagine a woman's calculations opening up the sky, the sun's orbit but a mole on the lip of solar clustered nipple. How she spilled the milk from the glass of her astronomer eye, knowing it would feed another hunger in another womb of time.

Mathematics were just foreplay. There is nothing wrong with being easy. Any man can scribble odes to flatter a goddess of the moon. She turned her garden into laboratory to decipher the secret turning of the stars. Behind the ecliptic strung-up crystal, she glimpsed her face in the lunar mirror's gleam.

Infinite planets. Her endless ether. There are those whose greatness grows in shadow, whose outer limits the spotting of blood cannot contain.

Wang Zhenyi (王貞儀, 1768–1797)
was an astronomer, mathematician, and
poet of the Qing Dynasty in China.
Self-taught and tenacious, she
transcended her time's feudal restrictions
on women, making innovative ideas
more accessible to all. Like the stars, she
is a rebel hero of limitless creativity that
my family looks up to.

Time Travels of the Older American Poet

C. W. Emerson

Today coming home after seeing
    The Surrealistic Adventures of Women Artists,
        I tripped and fell into a hole of sky,

tumbled up, and landed
        at the Locke Insulator Company,
Victor, New York, circa 1903.

I saw my grandfather, James, a baby
    held in the arms of his brother Fred,
        their father in his basement laboratory

mixing silica, filling beakers, stealing heat
        from Great-Grandmother's oven
long past a decent hour of the night.

Great-Grandfather Locke and Sons
    molded their molten glass
        into green and purple domes—

thick, smooth, helmet-headed—
        to perch atop telephone poles
          and line the railroads
of a nation newly on the move.

These Irish, these unschooled,
    these pre-autistic geniuses:

My heart is linked to their hearts
    by something like the cord
        that links *The Two Fridas,*

both sitting earthbound, politely, in chairs,
        their glistening aortas exposed.

Fred M. Locke (1861–1930) invented the porcelain insulator, used
to protect the electrical current of a power line. His factory
manufactured millions of porcelain insulators, and his glass
formulas are still in use today for Pyrex cookware, glass stovetops,
and Space Shuttle windows. He was my great-grandfather.

The Infectious Irony of Ignaz Semmelweis

Abbey Willman

August 1865, Vienna

I should have known it would kill me / in this asylum / this sanitary —
/ this sanitarium / all I can see past the blood — / past the guards / past
the rods beating me bloody — / the ward on my first rounds / oh God!
the never-ending sound / the dreadful pealing bell / held by drifting Priest
/ haunting the hallways / the smell of rot and iron / lingering /

on all — on all those —

how could I not see it sooner? / the phantom of the fever / so nasal thick
/ sticky on fingers / how could I not / see the gentlemen sneer as I taught
them how? / here is a bit / chlorinated lime destroys it / citrus fresh and
caustic quick / and so suggestive / how could I hint / a learnéd doctor as
putrid sick? /

after — after-all —

it will really kill me now / on crusted rods striking — / the smell of iron
— / copper / stiff and liquid / striking — / stricken — / on crusted
scalpel / my friend pricked his fingertip / my friend gone childbed / like
— like all those — / no baby to rush for / in cadaver birthing cadaver /
and without his grave / how could I have known / I couldn't have saved /

all those mothers!

Oh Mother! / my last call / my last blood pours now / onward, elsewhere
/ a world awaits where men put the lives of women above reputation /
they put no lives in such / involuntary placement / in such a sanitary —
/ in a new world / where my solution floods / oh Mother! no more blood!
/ buckets line every theater / every hand soaked with lime / so scentless
and clear / and my hands / and my hands are clean

> **Ignaz Semmelweis (1818–1865)** was a clinician who discovered that
> doctors examining cadavers would afterward infect women during
> childbirth and surmised that disinfecting the doctors' hands led to a
> decrease in puerperal fever deaths. When he tried to pioneer handwashing,
> however, he was mocked, placed in an asylum, and beaten. Many scholars
> believe he died from an infection brought on by the beating.

The Mousehouse

Kathleen R. Gilbert

Art Deco Buffalo City Hall, 21st floor
in your white lab coat you peer through an oil
immersion microscope for parasites:
cryptosporidium, schistosomes, filaria, leishmania.

You pause, stand, and gaze out: Lake Erie
iron gray with a winter storm coming,
look toward Black Rock and the lighthouse.

Cynthia, colleague and cohort, a friendly
face in a sea of men, comes in from the Milk
and Water Lab. Her next vacation plan:
a tramp freighter to Egypt on the Nile.

You, who have traveled from the farm in Alberta
to the States; from Depression to Recession;
from daughter, to mother; nowhere else, are envious.

Now a dog's skull to open, a brain to dissect,
slicing tissue samples of Negri bodies; prepping
injections for the mice to detect rabies.

You open the door to a closet full of cages.
Mice, hundreds, some with picric yellow painted stripes
indicating they were injected, squeak; the rancid odor,
fetid smell of rodent fur, pours into your nostrils.

Later you will bring one mouse home to me, your
sixteen-year-old daughter, to chloroform, cut,
extract the heart, keeping it beating with a salt solution
on the kitchen table. You want me to be a surgeon.

Scalpel in shaking hand, I realize I don't have
eyesight or steadiness to fulfill that dream; but
with you in mind, I will see rivers of five continents.

Julia Mary O'Callaghan Rumrich (1921–2007) battled illness and
promoted health in her post as Senior Microbiologist and Head of
the Rabies Lab for the Erie County (New York) Department of
Health. She contemporaneously served as clinical instructor of
parasitology at the Medical School of SUNY Buffalo. She was a
wife and a mother of five children, and I am one of them.

The Comet Hunters

Ellen Goldstein

This fact proves the great error of those scientific men
who figure ... a comet is but a flimsy affair ...
for here was a strong compact house—
albeit a small one—built entirely of them.
—Edward Emerson Barnard,
a comet hunter who used the $200 prize money
for every comet he found to build a house

I was raised in a house of comets,
a father tongue of scientific chatter:
celestial mechanics, dark matter,
Maxwell's equations, the obliquity
of the ecliptic, incomprehensible
as the night sky.

Against their mother's wishes, Caroline Herschel sneaked to the roof
with her brother to sweep the sky for comets,
rich patches of light, a sudden revolution
sliding between their horizons.
William taught Caroline to divine comets,
not dinner, twenty-three fragments of ice and rock
caught in the teeth of the stars. They stayed out
until the first veins of dawn dimmed
the slowly unfolding history of the universe.

My father believed the history of the universe was told
in magnetism. He charted the paths of minor planets
over thousands of years as they crossed and collided
at the edge of Jupiter's reach, an icy high-tide line.
Their orbits bloomed on his screen in complicated flowers.
Aren't they beautiful? I think I could sell them as art.

Charles Messier fell in love at seventeen.
Every night he went out and searched for comets
with his new glass telescope, but the sky was riddled
with false lights. Star clusters and nebulae
mimicked the pulse of his beloveds.
Fed up, he wrote a catalogue
of disappointments, a book of sluggish systems
that now bear his name, the Messier Objects.

Maria Mitchell slipped away
from a family tea to scan
the sky, one blur of light
spilled between the familiar
footsteps of the stars. This night,
her misplaced light led to a medal
from a Danish king, and a job
teaching, her sleeping couch
tucked into the dome room
at Vassar's new observatory
her bootsteps crossed all night.

Carolyn Shoemaker raised three children
in towns where streetlights muted the sky,
then followed her husband to Palomar.
In the mountains, darkness changed
with the hour. Carolyn watched starlight fall
onto her film. Waking up
in the afternoons, she felt daylight
fizz around her hands as she compared
the films, searching for a smudge
of light, a crumb of iron traveling faster,
closer than the stars. When she found one,
she called out to her husband:
It makes me want to dance.

Surrounded by astronomers in Zehmer Hall,
my father and I cheered as Shoemaker-Levy 9,
a broken chain of comets, crashed into Jupiter.
On the huge TV, we could see impacts of fragment C
rotating in concert, twin bitemarks
at infrared wavelengths.

When Ye Quanzhi was seven, he thought he discovered
Comet Hale-Bopp, but two Americans
had spotted it first. In college,
he found green Comet Lulin,
still composed of the origins
of the universe. (Quanzhi called himself
Lulin's boyfriend, and cut his hair
in the shape of her anti-tail.) Cyanogenic
and carbon gases peeled
from Lulin's icy face as it careened
backward, for the first time, toward the sun.

> My father, **Samuel J. Goldstein, Jr. (1925–2000)**,
> was an astronomer who hunted Trojan asteroids
> and loved to show his daughters the stars. Two of
> the most prominent comet hunters in history are
> women: **Caroline Herschel (1750–1848)** and
> **Carolyn Shoemaker (b. 1929)**. Finding comets is
> an accessible science, requiring only long hours
> observing the night sky. The solitude and
> dedication reminds me of the act of writing.

Edward Emerson Barnard (1857–1923)
Caroline Herschel (1750–1848)
William Herschel (1738–1822)
Charles Messier (1730–1817)
Maria Mitchell (1818–1889)
Carolyn Shoemaker (b. 1929)
Ye Quanzhi (叶泉志, b. 1989)

033: Whooping Cough

Carrie Purcell Kahler

I.

anno domini 1484
tosse cattiva
preghiamo a madonna della tosse
grace for our children
we pray in the chapel

a stream runs under the chapel
the water from the stream
and the steam from our breath
coats frescos in salt and gypsum

the frescos of madonna's death
are mute while we pray
and our children whoop

II.

1930 to 1939
fifty thousand children die
by pertussis percussive blood vessels
burst in brains by force of coughing

pearl and grace
begin in 1934 a vaccine
trials by kerosene
collecting samples from
the dirt poor the city poor
the tidy poor some few not quite poor
of western michigan
the pta peeds clinics
those doctors who agree
volunteers in tears from strangled coughs
agree to keep records of strangled coughs
and the super says
"go ahead
if it amuses you"

in the lab after hours after petri and cough plates
and never enough funding then
mrs. eleanor roosevelt
accepts your invitation
mrs. eleanor roosevelt
arranges funding for admin positions
cataloguing symptom onsets
setting aside records that cannot count
setting event timing system
setting follow ups
correctly matching controls so
pearl and grace test successful

by 1984 whooping deaths down to seven

III.

now we do not need to beg madonna
about the cough
now there is no cough
now gypsum covers her quiet face
we clean her
and move her
to a storage space

o mother
we prayed for grace here
four hundred fifty years
why did you delay

Grace Eldering (1900–1988) and
Pearl Kendrick (1890–1980)
developed the first whooping
cough vaccine during the Great
Depression after completing daily
water and milk analyses. They
helped establish rules for
conducting largescale field studies
and developed partnerships with
the community to identify, test,
and treat children near their
Grand Rapids lab.

Oh Be a Fine Girl, Kiss Me

Alyssa D. Ross

She wore her hair frenzied in the pandemonium
of the big bang, innumerable strands extending
and ending. With a name made to move,
she was bound to measure
the bright stellar banter.

Immersed in the spectral outbursts
of a universe that she could not hear,
her soft, stifled ears never stopping
pursuit of interstellar career.

Gaining a newfound sight
to catalog the cosmos,
creating the Scheme, nothing wicked
but a cosmological classification.

The eldest daughter made independent
by the environment. Taking her mother's advice,
she chased the dotted constellations, once traced
with long finger guiding little hand.

Toting her Blair box around Europe,
she began to be another.
As her ears hardened,
art unfurled in the photographs,

> **Annie Jump Cannon (1863–1941)** was an American Astronomer who worked for the Harvard Observatory under **Edward Charles Pickering (1846–1919)**. Despite being nearly deaf, Cannon would become the first woman to hold an honorary doctorate from Oxford University for her work on stellar classification, the first organization of stars based on their temperatures and spectral types.

images of grayscale.
Lost in the darkroom,
buried in its negative beauty,
she pretended to become another.

It was not a photograph, but the subjects
that gave her ruddy cheeks their color.
Pictures of the far, longing lights
still spoke to her with a silver whisper.

When her hearing was smothered,
like a flame snuffed out by blankets of time,
she became another.

Annie Jump Cannon's mnemonic for remembering the spectral classes, OBAFGKM, was: *Oh Be a Fine Girl, Kiss Me.* This sequence is used to identify stars from the coolest (O type) to the hottest (M type). Each letter class is then subdivided into a numeric score ranging from 0-9 (hottest to coolest). Thus, a star labeled M0 would represent one of the hottest stars, whereas O9 would represent one of the coolest.

D'Ye Know Me?

Neil Rhind

To Bob Ball,
first to tell me the good news,
February 2017

Time flies like an arrow; fruit flies, like the axolotl
Have lent us landmarks in the mapping of genomes
With flies, the nuclear marrow of these laboratory cattle
Was chosen as it's small: eight chromosomes

Matched in four pairs. They're also very fecund,
Breed with speed, quick to mature and to gestate
And hatch their heirs, hence why Nobels beckoned
For eight separate projects based on them to date.

It's not the ease of reading them that chose
Axolotls; their genome's size is ten times ours.
We got the ABCs of their multibillion base pair prose
In the hope it helps us probe their superpowers.

Nearly any wound gets better; soon, we hope, to be explained
By the thirty-two billion letters twisted round their nuclear chain.

Elly M. Tanaka (b. 1965), Michael Hiller, Gene W. Myers (b. 1953), Siegfried Schloißnig, et al., were the first team to map the axolotl genome. At thirty-two billion base pairs, this was the longest species genome yet mapped. There is an added poignancy, as the axolotl has been declared extinct in the wild yet thrives in captivity due to its popularity as a laboratory animal.

Star-Taker

Elosham Vog

He called it a dream, but it wasn't—
more a vision, a meld of memory,
science, and fear. He sold it anyway:

Himself a small child amongst glaciers,
eye pressed against convex lens,
charting the course of Earth around sun

and the magnetic pull of the moon.
His mother a witch, father a mercenary
absence. The boy no stranger to turning tides.

For solace he imagined lunar landscapes,
turned his mind to the mundane earth
only when he felt it shaking beneath him,

when the witch staked out in icy corrie
sang or sobbed too loud to ignore.
He'd never really known her;

he'd known her too well, felt the tendrils
of herbs from her bag twine round his brow,
the prick of bone needles in skin,

the chill of her gaze as he numbered the stars.
He inked her into his maps, the sun a rival
to the flames that circled her,

that licked, caressed, beckoned,
so hot parchment singed as he drew.
He couldn't reach her, couldn't risk

singemark scars on tender skin,
the chance of hysteric eruption, of slipping
or sliding in the warm melt of skirting glaciers

formed from frozen tears. He cried
with her, felt the burn of salt
on wind-chapped cheeks, hard eyes

of the town holding him back
even as the flood crested at their doors
and threatened to shake sheilings loose.

Earth-mother, he sang. Moon-tether,
awash in your tears. Be still the storm,
temper the flame. I wash in your tears.

And still they flowed, gathering force
and gravel, scraps of lumber and old ashes,
dust and debris, a deluge of mud

swallowing everything in its wake.

Johannes Kepler (1571–1630) was an
influential astronomer, mathematician,
and optical researcher. It is believed
that the inclusion of a witch mother in
Kepler's *Somnium* (which is both
science-fiction novel and serious treatise
on lunar astronomy in defense of
heliocentrism) was an influence in the
accusation and imprisonment of
Kepler's own mother for witchcraft.

Never Doubt

Tori Grant Welhouse

Hers was the idea of going
to the field for answers.
Learning from a south sea island
the currency of human behavior.
The imperative of her travel,
marriages, love, anthropology.
There was no such thing as random.
Or spontaneous. Or primitive.
Nature and nurture share five
letters. It has to start somewhere—
ties that bind, continue, get carried
from one person to the next.
We are born; we die. In between
we create each other, ritual, reasons
to depend, defend, befriend the
phases of ourselves, humanity.

The desire to observe was a gift—
the care, the generosity. We can
always learn from each other.
Why was she criticized? Nobody
ever gets it completely right.
We can't unskew our perspective.
We see each other but remain
utterly mysterious, dreaming the
same shadowy dreams we can't
explain. She was a woman, of course.
That frame for building thought already
half-built. *Coming of Age in Samoa*
was a bestseller, skyful of stars,
first glimpse of a range of thought
too big, perhaps, for a box,
nevermind choosing a new future,
or sharing the heavens.

Margaret Mead (1901–1978)
was an American
anthropologist and human
rights activist. She studied the
connection between culture
and personality by living and
interacting with the peoples of
Oceania, and she made
anthropology accessible to
laypeople. The poem title
references her famous quote:
"Never doubt that a small
group of thoughtful,
committed citizens can
change the world; indeed, it's
the only thing that ever has."

Pharmaceutical Chemistry

Leah Bishop

My daddy used to lie belly down
on the rug with me, connecting
hexagons in my sketchbook.

That's sugar, he told me. *That's
beer. That's insulin.* All this
he created like he created

me. I giggled, and we boiled
spaghetti, safety goggles
strapped on. He gave me

a microscope, and I made slides
of my saliva, to my mother's
dismay. He gave me his textbook

for my eighth birthday, signed
by some old man. I'd wanted
earrings. He gave me

evolution and secular Sunday
school classes and the notion
that sneakers could go with jeans

and his genes. He kissed
my scientific skull and knew
that soon a valve within it would pop

and panic would flood
my cavities, burn ulcers
in my stomach walls, and keep me

home on weekdays. He knew
I'd want him to make my insides
into slides and draw new molecules

to inject in my afflictions, but he would hide
my microscope, lie beside
my convulsions, put lemon drops

in my pillbox and essential oils
in my cabinet. He'd never open
my test results, knowing

they'd be negative, like his.

> **My Father (b. 1965)** is an
> organic chemist who works in
> drug discovery. Besides
> chemistry, he is famous for his
> beer-brewing parties, his
> willingness to dance in public
> despite his family's consensus
> that he should not do so, and
> his adoration for my mother.

Author Biographies

Kathy Ackerman

has published one full-length poetry book, *Coal River Road* (Livingston Press, University of West Alabama), and three chapbooks. Her poems have appeared in numerous journals, including *Southern Poetry Review* and *North American Review*. She is Writer-in-Residence and Dean of Arts and Sciences at Isothermal Community College in Spindale, North Carolina.

Leah Angstman

is a historian, transplanted Midwesterner, and board member of a Colorado historical commission. She serves as editor-in-chief for Alternating Current and *The Coil*, a reviewer for *Publishers Weekly*, and a proofreader for *Pacific Standard*. Her work has appeared in *Los Angeles Review of Books*, *Electric Literature*, *Slice*, and elsewhere. Find her at leahangstman.com and on social media as @leahangstman.

Tani Arness

lives in Albuquerque, New Mexico. Her poems can be found in the collection *Tzimtzum* from Mercury Heartlink Publishing. Her poetry can also be found in numerous literary magazines, including *North American Review*, *Rhino*, *Bosque*, *Malpaís Review*, and *Crab Orchard Review*. Her website is tani-arness.com.

Harvey Aughton

is a writer based in New Zealand. He has completed anthropology and psychology degrees since working as an outdoor instructor. His work has previously been published in *Takahē Magazine*, *The Dawntreader*, and *Mayhem Literary Journal*.

Carol Barrett

holds doctorates in both clinical psychology and creative writing. She coordinates the Creative Writing Certificate Program at Union Institute and University. Her books include *Calling in the Bones* (which won the Snyder Prize from Ashland Poetry Press), *Drawing Lessons* (Finishing Line Press), and *Pansies* (creative nonfiction, Sonder Press).

Matilda Berke

is a sophomore from Pasadena, California, double-majoring in International Relations-Economics and English at Wellesley College. She has been recognized by *The Adroit Journal*, YoungArts, the Scholastic Art and Writing Awards, the Los Angeles Tomorrow Prize, and the Los Angeles Youth Poet Laureate competition, among others. Find more of her writing at *Pedestal Magazine* and *Up the Staircase Quarterly*.

Leah Bishop

is an emerging queer author of poetry and fiction. Her work has been featured by Gertrude Press, Lycan Valley Press Publications, the Southern Literary Festival, and *The Coil*. She currently lives and works in Tucson, Arizona.

Amanda Bloom

has work published or forthcoming in *The Atlantic, The Rumpus, The Yale Review, The Cardiff Review,* and elsewhere. She was a 2017 Pushcart Prize nominee and a fiction finalist in the 2018 *Iowa Review* Awards. Amanda is a fiction editor at the *New Haven Review.*

Carl Boon

is the author of *Places & Names,* coming in 2019 from The Nasiona Press. His poems have appeared in many journals and magazines, including *Posit* and *The Maine Review.* A Pushcart Prize nominee, he lives in Izmir, Turkey, and teaches courses in American literature at Dokuz Eylül University.

James Broschart

is retired from careers in classroom teaching, public television production, technical writing, and bookstore management. His poems have appeared in various publications, such as *Ars Medica, Artemis, Blueline, The Enigmatist,* and *Sociological Origins.* A collection of his poetry, *Old News,* was published by Finishing Line Press in 2018.

Brianna Bullen

is a writer and Deakin University PhD candidate writing about memory in science fiction. She has had work published in journals including *LiNQ, Aurealis, Voiceworks, Mascara,* and *Multiverse: An International Anthology of Science-Fiction Poetry.* She won the 2017 Apollo Bay short story competition.

Mackenzie Bush

is a queer writer living in Grand Rapids, Michigan, who writes about ghosts, cryptids, and the judges from *Chopped.* She likes blue nail polish, crystals, and watching figure skating. She is currently publishing queer romance novels cowritten under the name C. M. Valencourt.

Hannah Carr-Murphy

is a poet and musician from Waterloo, Iowa. Her poetry has appeared in *Common Ground Review, Presence: A Journal of Catholic Poetry,* and anthologies from Mammoth Books and Final Thursday Press. She holds degrees from University of Northern Iowa and University of Limerick, Ireland.

Alan Catlin

has been publishing for five decades. Among his many books and chapbooks, most recently, are the full-length book *Wild Beauty* (Future Cycle Press) and the ekphrastic chapbook *Three Farmers on the Way to a Dance* (Presa Press). He won the 2017 Slipstream Chapbook Award for his chapbook *Blue Velvet.*

Robin Chapman

is Professor emerita of Communication Sciences and Disorders at the University of Wisconsin-Madison. Her ninth book of poetry, *Six True Things* (Tebot Bach, 2016), poems about growing up in the scientists' town of Oak Ridge, Tennessee, received the Wisconsin Library Association's Outstanding Book of Poetry Award in 2017.

Catharina Coenen

is a German immigrant to Northwestern Pennsylvania, where she teaches college biology. Her creative work has appeared or is forthcoming in *Appalachian Heritage, The Christian Science Monitor, Bird's Thumb, Anastamos,* and elsewhere.

Sanda Moore Coleman

is a theater commentator for public radio and founder of the Wichita Fringe Festival, featuring original work by area high school playwrights. In 2011, she won the Maureen Egen prize in fiction from *Poets & Writers* magazine. Her poems have appeared in several print and online journals.

Heather Combe

was born in Edinburgh and now lives near London, where she works for a large university. She began writing poetry as a teenager and has continued while pursuing a career in science. She finds inspiration in long train journeys to Scotland, learning obscure medical terminology, and good whisky.

Jessica Conley

teaches Literature at The Steward School in Richmond, Virginia. She is also an MFA Poetry student at Virginia Commonwealth University, where she earned her BA in English and MA in Secondary English Education. She has been published in literary magazines such as *The Gordian Review* and *Glassworks Magazine.*

Mikaela Curry

is a published poet, performer, and community organizer living in eastern Kentucky. She regularly performs spoken word poetry that reflects her passion for equity, environmental health, and social justice. She holds advanced degrees in biological sciences and has worked as an environmental specialist, consultant, conservationist, and researcher.

Chase Dimock

is an English professor from Los Angeles and the managing editor of *As It Ought to Be Magazine.* He holds a PhD in Comparative Literature from the University of Illinois. His work has appeared in *College Literature, Lambda Literary Review, Hot Metal Bridge, Waccamaw,* and *Saw Palm.*

Caroline DuBois

has published works in an eclectic array of formats, from *Highlights High Five, Southern Poetry Review,* the Poetry in Motion Program, to *The Journal of the American Medical Association.* She lives in Nashville, Tennessee; works as a middle-school literacy coach; and enjoys birdwatching, playing soccer, and gardening.

C. W. Emerson

has had work appear in journals including *Atlanta Review, Crab Orchard Review, The American Journal of Poetry, Tupelo Quarterly,* and others. He was a recent finalist for the New Millennium Award for Poetry, the *New Ohio Review* Poetry Contest, the Two Sylvias Chapbook Prize, and the *New Letters* Prize for Poetry.

Jane Frank

is a writer from Brisbane, Australia, where she teaches in Creative Industries at Griffith University. Recent poems have appeared in *Takahē, Stilts Journal, Not Very Quiet, Algebra of Owls, Heroines* (Neo Perennial Press, 2018), and *Pale Fire: New Writings on the Moon* (Frogmore Press, 2019). Visit facebook.com/JaneFrankPoet; janefrankpoetry.wordpress.com.

Corinna German

writes with the Absaroka-Beartooth Wilderness over her shoulder. Her work has appeared in *Blood, Water, Wind, and Stone: An Anthology of Wyoming Writers* (Sastrugi Press), *Manifest West: Women of the West* (Western Press Books), and numerous literary journals. Find her at @corinnawriter on Twitter.

Emryse Geye

is a queer poet and chemistry graduate student from the Pacific Northwest, via Texas. When she's not dismantling traditional gender hierarchies in STEM fields, she can be found at your local Portland poetry slam. Read more of her work at emryse.com.

Megan Gieske

is a wandering poet. So far, she has taught and written poetry in nineteen countries. Last year, her poetry won an International Poetry Competition Merit Award from *Atlanta Review*. She is from Fredon, New Jersey. You can read more of her poems and follow her on social media at megangieske.com.

Kathleen R. Gilbert

is an award-winning poet published in collections such as *The Best of the Steel Toe Review, Swamp, The Community of Writers Poetry Review, Transfer, Anomalous,* and *Poiesis Review.* She also wrote a children's book, *Just Us Chickens.*

Ellen Goldstein

is the author of *Stuff Every Beer Snob Should Know* (Quirk Books, 2018) and the forthcoming *Writer's Field Journal* (Fox Chapel Publishing). Her poetry and essays have been published in a wide range of journals and anthologies. She lives, writes, and edits in Southern Vermont. Visit her website at crescenteditorial.com.

Robin Gow

has had poetry recently published in *Poetry, Tilde,* and *Let's Try This with the Lights On.* He is a graduate student and professor at Adelphi University pursing an MFA, and he coordinates social media for *Oyster River Pages.* He is a bisexual transgender man passionate about LGBT issues.

Peter J. Grieco

is a poet and composer living in Buffalo, New York, his native city. His poems have been published widely in print and online. He updates a poetry blog at pjgrieco.wordpress.com.

Liz Hart

is a full-time queer, mother, wife, and hobby farmer living in Oregon and constantly begging life for reasons. She has been published in *Oregon Humanities*, in *Line Zero*, and at Zoetic Press. Writing isn't everything, but it's the best something that there might be.

Carrie Purcell Kahler

writes mostly poetry. Her work has appeared or is forthcoming in *Image*, *Arcturus*, *District Lit*, *Hobart*, *DMQ Review*, and others. She manages events for *Poetry Northwest* and lives in Seattle with her husband and cat.

Charles Kersey

is a distributed systems analyst during the day and artist-humorist during his off-time. His poetry has appeared in *Candelabrum*, *WordART*, *Haikuniverse*, and other publications. His visual art is displayed in private galleries in Florida and the Netherlands. Find him on Twitter at @charleskersey.

Robert Kibble

is the son of a physics professor and an English teacher, so the union of science and English seems natural. His father, one of the six people who came up with the concept of the Higgs boson back in the 1960s, took him to a lecture at the Royal Society in London, where he heard Adam Hart-Davis defending Robert Hooke's legacy, and ... well ... something had to be done.

Anna Leahy

is the author of the nonfiction book *Tumor* (Bloomsbury) and the poetry collections *Aperture* (Shearsman) and *Constituents of Matter* (Kent State University Press). She directs the MFA in Creative Writing program at Chapman University and edits *TAB: The Journal of Poetry & Poetics*. See more at amleahy.com.

Michael H. Levin

is an environmental lawyer, solar energy developer, and writer based in Washington, D.C. His work has appeared in two chapbooks and dozens of periodicals and has received numerous poetry and feature journalism awards. Visit him at michaellevinpoetry.com.

Bryanna Licciardi

is a poet-slash-academic-advisor from Middle Tennessee (and yes, those things go together). She's a multi-Pushcart Prize nominee and has work in journals like *BlazeVox*, *Poetry Quarterly*, and *Peacock Journal*. Licciardi's chapbook, *Skin Splitting*, is out from Finishing Line Press. Visit her at bryannalicciardi.com.

Colleen Maynard

is a writer and artist. Her work has appeared in *Cold Mountain Review* and *Sand Journal*. Maynard was selected for the inaugural collaborative "Visual Pathology" with University of Texas Medical Branch and Galveston Art Center. She holds writing and painting majors from the Kansas City Art Institute.

Kindra McDonald

received her MFA from Queens University of Charlotte. She teaches poetry and is an adjunct writing professor and sometimes doctoral student. She is the author of the chapbooks *Concealed Weapons* and *Elements and Briars* and the poetry collections *Fossils* and *In the Meat Years*.

Ethan Milner

is a writer and a psychotherapist living in Oregon. He works at a school for youth with special needs, and his work has appeared in *The Offing*, *Decomp*, *Dream Pop*, and other journals. He can be found on Twitter at @confident_memes.

Ilan Mochari

is the author of the Pushcart-nominated novel *Zinsky the Obscure* (Fomite, 2013). His poems and short stories have appeared or are forthcoming in *McSweeney's*, *Hobart*, *J Journal*, *Valparaiso Fiction Review*, and elsewhere.

Sarah Mooney

is a writer living in Queens, New York. "Bathtub" is her first published poem.

Wilda Morris

is Workshop Chair of Poets & Patrons and former president of the Illinois State Poetry Society. Her second book is *Pequod Poems: Gamming with Moby-Dick*. Wilda is widely published and has won awards for free and formal verse and haiku. Find her monthly contest for poets at wildamorris.blogspot.com.

Linnea Nelson

is a writer based in Richmond, Virginia. Her poetry has appeared in *Rattle*, *Rappahannock Review*, *The Adirondack Review*, *San Pedro River Review*, and *Tule Review*, among other journals and anthologies. She is an editor for Cloudbank Books and holds an MFA from Oregon State University.

Monica Ong

is the author of *Silent Anatomies* (2015), winner of the Kore Press First Book Award in poetry. A Kundiman poetry fellow and MFA graduate in Digital Media at the Rhode Island School of Design, she currently serves as the User Experience Designer at the Yale Digital Humanities Laboratory.

David Pring-Mill

is a writer and filmmaker. His poems have been published in *Poetry Quarterly*, *Boston Literary Magazine*, *Crack the Spine*, *Five:2:One*, and elsewhere. He is also the editor of the literary anthology *Tiny Moments*. Find out more at pring-mill.com.

Neil Rhind

received his doctorate from Edinburgh and has contributed to *The Scottish Literary Review*, *The International Review of Scottish Studies*, the *International Journal of Scottish Literature*, and others. His poorly-edited religious meditation, *What Sort of Pagan Does That?* is available online. He has bred many an axolotl.

Alyssa D. Ross

was born in Guntersville, Alabama, but spent over a decade in Northern Virginia. She holds an MFA from George Mason University and a PhD from Auburn University. Dr. Ross currently teaches writing and literature at Auburn University, in community outreach, and in the Alabama corrections system.

Sara Sams

is a poet, essayist, and translator from Oak Ridge, Tennessee. She currently works as an instructor for Arizona State University's College of Integrative Sciences and Arts, where she provides faculty support to the *Superstition Review*. She is a graduate of Davidson College (BA) and Arizona State University (MFA).

Lorraine Schein

is a New York writer. Her work has appeared in *Strange Horizons, Vice Terraform, Syntax and Salt*, and *New Letters* and in the anthologies *Multiverse, Tragedy Queens: Stories Inspired by Lana del Rey & Sylvia Plath*, and *Aphrodite Terra*. *The Futurist's Mistress*, her poetry book, is available from mayapplepress.com.

Roger Sippl

studied creative writing at UC Irvine, UC Berkeley, and Stanford Continuing Studies. He has enjoyed being published in a few dozen online and print literary journals and anthologies, including *The Ocean State Review*. He was also a successful pioneer in Silicon Valley. See what he's been doing at rogersippl.com.

Bruce Taylor

has had poetry appear in *Able Muse, The American Poetry Journal, The Chicago Review, Cortland Review, The Formalist, Light, The Nation, The New York Quarterly, Poetry*, and *Rattle*. Find him at people.uwec.edu/taylorb.

Armin Tolentino

is the author of the poetry collection *We Meant to Bring It Home Alive* (Alternating Current Press). He studied chemistry in college and currently lives in Vancouver, Washington.

Sherre Vernon

is an educator, a poet, and a believer in the mystical power of words. Sherre has written two award-winning chapbooks: *Green Ink Wings*, her postmodern novella, and *The Name Is Perilous*, a poetry chapbook.

Elosham Vog

is a poet and Forward Prize nominee. His poem in this collection is an excerpt from his verse novel, *Volcano*. Other *Volcano* poems have appeared in a variety of (mostly UK-based) publications, including *The Interpreter's House, The Missing Slate, The Istanbul Review*, and *Lighthouse*.

Tori Grant Welhouse

is a poet, photographer, and active volunteer with Wisconsin Fellowship of Poets. She earned an MFA with Antioch University and has a chapbook, *Canned*, with Finishing Line Press. Her poetry has most recently appeared in *Mayday Magazine*, in *New Midwest Poetry*, and at Quill's Edge Press. More at torigrantwelhouse.com.

Abbey Willman

is a graduate of the University of Washington in Seattle, with studies in philosophy and American Sign Language. Her emphasis was specifically on the history and philosophy of science. She plans on becoming a K-12 teacher and spends much of her time reading, writing, and crying over long-dead historical figures.

Christie Wilson

lives in Illinois. Her work appears in *Atticus Review*, *Cheap Pop*, *Driftwood Press*, and *New World Writing*, among other publications. For information about her work or to contact her, please visit christiewilson.net.

Steve Wilson

lives and works in San Marcos, Texas, where he teaches at Texas State University. His work has appeared in journals and anthologies nationwide, and he is the author of five poetry collections, including *Lose to Find* (2018) and *The Reaches* (2019).

Kaylyn Wingo

is a retired paralegal living in Michigan, where she is a member of the Waterford Township Public Library's Poetry Writers' Workshop. She has been published in *Poetry Leaves* and *Voice of Eve*.

Amy Wright

is the author of two poetry books, one poetry collaboration, and six chapbooks, including the forthcoming prose chapbook *Think I'll Go Eat a Worm*. Her poems have appeared in *Kenyon Review*, *Appalachian Heritage*, *Smartish Pace*, and *Southern Poetry Anthology* Volumes III and VI.

Acknowledgments

Alternating Current Press wishes to acknowledge the following publications where poems from this anthology first appeared:

"Rutherford Discovers His Own Hollowness" was previously published in *Verseweavers*.

"Kepler's Last Autumn" was previously published in *High Plains Literary Review*.

"The Robbery of Rosalind Franklin" was previously published in *The Women's Review of Books*.

"De Motu Cordis (On the Motion of the Heart)" was previously published in *Sentinel Literary Quarterly*.

"Falling Up" was previously published in the poetry book *Old News* (Finishing Line Press, 2018).

"Hedy Lamarr and George Antheil Invent Spread-Spectrum Broadcasting" was previously published in *The Antigonish Review*.

"The Habits of Light" was previously published in *Comstock Review* and in the poetry book *Aperture* (Shearsman, 2017), and it was read by Ann Hamilton at The Universe in Verse 2017; view the reading at vimeo.com/262836574.

"Loxodonta Africana, Loxodonta Cyclotis" was previously published in *Alegrarse*.

"April 19, 1906" was previously published in *The Broad River Review*.

"Resurrection" was previously published in *Out of Line*.

"Milk" was previously published in *Poet Lore*.

"Flight" was previously published in the poetry book *In Other Words* (Upriver Press, 2014).

"Woman's Place in the Universe" was previously published in an alternative layout format in *Waxwing Literary Magazine*.

"Time Travels of the Older American Poet" was previously published in *Wild Violet*.

"The Mousehouse" was previously published in *Transfer*.

"Star-Taker" was previously published in *The Fenland Reed*.

Endnotes & Bibliographies

"Domestication" contains italicized lines at the beginning and end of the poem that come from *The Little Prince* by Antoine de Saint-Exupéry.

"Petite Curies" author note: Marie Curie's long-awaited Radium Institute in Paris was complete in 1914. But when Germany invaded France, the researchers and the patients were at the Front. Marie convinced automobile manufacturers to transform cars into vans carrying portable X-Ray equipment for use on the battlefield. Then she learned to drive. Her daughter Irène and she, unprotected from the radiation themselves, saved the lives of thousands of soldiers by providing this crucial service to wartime surgeons. The soldiers dubbed the cars Petite Curies.

"Ève of the Radium Eyes" was a phrase coined by members of the press who were infatuated by Ève Curie's beauty. Mé was a term of endearment used by Marie Curie's daughters to refer to her.

"St. Petersburg, 1969" contains an epigraph in Russian that comes from A. S. Pushkin's poem "The Bronze Horseman."

"De Motu Cordis (On the Motion of the Heart)" contains an epigraph that references the edition of William Harvey's *On the Motion of the Heart and Blood in Animals* published by The Harvard Classics, 1909–1914.

"Alternatives to Spruce" references the following publications: *The Caste War of Yucatán* by Nelson A. Reed, *The Great American Chewing Gum Book* by Robert Hendrickson, *Bubblemania* by Lee Wardlaw, *Chicle: The Chewing Gum of the Americas from the Ancient Maya to William Wrigley* by Jennifer P. Mathews, *Chewing Gum: The Fortunes of Taste* by Michael Redclift, *The Bubble-Gum Card War* by Dean Hanley, *Pop! The Invention of Bubble Gum* by Meghan McCarthy, and *The Chewing Gum Book* by Robert Young.

"XVII. Misinterpretations are not so much Illusions as Evasions (233)" is from a series of verses by the author that reimagines and responds to the dream texts and commentaries of Sigmund Freud as presented in his *The Interpretation of Dreams*. The number in parentheses that accompanies the title refers to the page number in the 1955 Basic Books edition, where the text related to this "misinterpretation" begins.

"The Red-Shouldered Vanga" references the article "Seven Women Who Made the World Better for Birds and People," Emily Silber, March 31, 2016, audubon.org.

"On the Nature of Matter" references: 1.) *The Other Einstein* by Marie Benedict (Sourcebooks, 2016); 2.) *Symphony No. 38: Prague*, and *Concerto for Flute and Harp* by Wolfgang Amadeus Mozart, Detroit Symphony Orchestra, Leonard Slatkin: Music Director, Mozart Festival, February 2017; 3.) *Genius*, National Geographic, channel.nationalgeographic.com /genius.

"I watched you die—" borrows famous lines from David Bowie's song "Space Oddity."

"For Dahlia" contains a list of victims of the École Polytechnique massacre that references: 1.) *Montreal Gazette* (December 5, 2014), "Remembering the Polytechnique victims"; 2.) *CBC Montreal*, M. Dalton (December 1, 2014), "Remember the 14."

"Woman's Place in the Universe" is presented here as a text-only version of a visual poem previously published in the Spring 2018 issue of *Waxwing Literary Magazine* and based on an illustration of the Diagram of the Stellar Universe in *Man's Place in the Universe* by Alfred R. Wallace, McClure, Phillips & Co.: 1903.

"Oh Be a Fine Girl, Kiss Me" references in the third stanza: Cannon, Annie Jump, "Spectra Having Bright Lines," *Annals of the Astronomical Observatory of Harvard College*, v. 76, no. 3, Cambridge, Mass.: The Observatory, 1916, pages 19–42. The footnote references: Kass-Simon, Gabriele, *Women of Science: Righting the Record*, Vol. 813, Indiana University Press, 1993, print page 91, Pamela Mack.

Colophon

The edition you are holding is the First Edition of this publication.

The title font is Teutonic, created by Peter Wiegel. The cursive font is Himdath, created by Olex Studio and RabbitType. The Alternating Current Press logo is Portmanteau, created by JLH Fonts. All other text is Calisto MT. All fonts are used with permission; all rights reserved.

The Alternating Current lightbulb logo was created by Leah Angstman, ©2013, 2019 Alternating Current. The atom divider is in the public domain, courtesy of ClipArtMax.

Front cover artwork: "Make Science." Artwork by Kelsey Thompson. Property of and ©2014, 2019 Kelsey Thompson. Based on "Absinthe Robette" by Henri Privat-Livemont, 1896. Visit kelseythompsonart.com. Used with permission; all rights reserved.

Back cover artwork: "The Architect." Artwork by Loui Jover. Property of and ©2019 Loui Jover. Find him on Instagram at @louijover, on Facebook at facebook.com/lojoverart and at saatchiart.com/louijover. Used with permission; all rights reserved.

All other material was created, designed, modified, or edited by Leah Angstman. All material is used with permission; all rights reserved.

Other Works from
Alternating Current Press

All of these books (and more) are available at Alternating Current's
website: press.alternatingcurrentarts.com.

alternatingcurrentarts.com

Made in the USA
Monee, IL
08 October 2021